Alastair
Sawday's

Special Places
to Stay

Wales

First edition
Copyright © 2010 Alastair Sawday
Publishing Co. Ltd

Published in 2010

Alastair Sawday Publishing Co. Ltd,
The Old Farmyard, Yanley Lane,
Long Ashton, Bristol BS41 9LR, UK
Tel: +44 (0)1275 395430
Fax: +44 (0)1275 393388
Email: info@sawdays.co.uk
Web: www.sawdays.co.uk

The Globe Pequot Press,
P. O. Box 480, Guilford,
Connecticut 06437, USA
Tel: +1 203 458 4500
Fax: +1 203 458 4601
Email: info@globepequot.com
Web: www.globepequot.com

Maps: Maidenhead Cartographic Services
Printing: Butler, Tanner & Dennis
UK distribution: Penguin UK, London

ISBN-13: 978-1-906136-49-9

Alastair Sawday has asserted his right to
be identified as the author of this work.

*We have made every effort to ensure the
accuracy of the information in this book at
the time of going to press. However, we cannot
accept any responsibility for any loss, injury
or inconvenience resulting from the use of
information contained therein.*

Cover design: Company X, Bristol.
Cover photo credits. Thanks to:
1. The Old Rectory, entry 40 2. www.istockphoto.com 3. www.paulgroom.com
Photo right: Visit Wales

Contents

The buildings

Beautiful as they were, our old offices leaked heat, used electricity to heat water and rooms, flooded spaces with light to illuminate one person, and were not ours to alter. So in 2005 we created our own eco-offices by converting some old barns to create a low-emissions building. We made the building energy-efficient through a variety of innovative and energy-saving building techniques, described below.

Insulation We went to great lengths to ensure that very little heat will escape, by:

• laying insulating board 90mm thick immediately under the roof tiles and on the floor

• lining the whole of the inside of the building with plastic sheeting to ensure air-tightness

• fixing further insulation underneath the roof and between the rafters

• fixing insulated plaster-board to add yet another layer of insulation.

All this means we are insulated for the Arctic, and almost totally air-tight.

Heating We installed a wood-pellet boiler from Austria, in order to be largely fossil-fuel free. The pellets are made from compressed sawdust, a waste product from timber mills that work only with sustainably managed forests. The heat is conveyed by water, throughout the building, via an under-floor system.

Water We installed a 6000-litre tank to collect rainwater from the roofs. This is pumped back, via an ultra-violet filter, to the lavatories, showers and basins. There are two solar thermal panels on the roof providing heat to the one (massively insulated) hot-water cylinder.

Lighting We have a carefully planned mix of low-energy lighting: task lighting and up-lighting. We also installed three sun-pipes – polished aluminium tubes that reflect the outside light down to chosen areas of the building.

Electricity All our electricity has long come from the Good Energy company and is 100% renewable.

Materials Virtually all materials are non-toxic or natural. Our carpets, for example, are made from (80%) Herdwick sheep-wool from National Trust farms in the Lake District.

Doors and windows Outside doors and new windows are wooden, double-glazed and beautifully constructed in Norway. Old windows have been double-glazed.

We have a building we are proud of, and architects and designers are fascinated by. But best of all, we are now in a better position to encourage our owners and readers to take sustainability more seriously.

What we do

Besides having moved the business to a low-carbon building, the company works in a number of ways to reduce its overall environmental footprint.

Our footprint We measure our footprint annually and use this information to find ways of reducing our environmental impact. To help address unavoidable carbon emissions

Photo: Tom Germain

we try to put something back: since 2006 we have supported SCAD, an organisation that works with villagers in India to create genuinely sustainable development.

Our office Nearly all of our office waste is recycled; kitchen waste is composted and used in the office vegetable garden. Left-over fruit and veg goes to the locally-owned pigs across the lane, who have recently been joined by chickens rescued from battery farms. Organic and fairtrade basic provisions are used in the staff kitchen and at in-house events, and green cleaning products are used throughout the office.

For many years we have been 'greening' the business in different ways. Our aim is to reduce our environmental footprint as far as possible, and almost every decision we make takes into account the environmental implications. In recognition of our efforts we won a Business Commitment to the Environment Award in 2005, and in 2006 a Queen's Award for Enterprise in the Sustainable Development category. In that year Alastair was voted ITN's 'Eco Hero'. In 2009 we were given the South West C+ Carbon Positive Consumer Choices Award for our Ethical Collection.

In 2008 and again in 2009 we won the IPG Environmental Award. In 2009 we were also the IPG overall Independent Publisher and Trade Publisher of the Year. The judging panel were effusive in their praise, stating: "With green issues currently at the forefront of publishers' minds, Alastair Sawday Publishing was singled out in this category as a model for all independents to follow. Its efforts to reduce waste in its office and supply chain have reduced the company's environmental impact, and it works closely with staff to identify more areas of improvement. Here is a publisher who lives and breathes green. Alastair Sawday has all the right principles and is clearly committed to improving its practice further."

We don't plan to pursue growth for growth's sake. The Sawday's name – and thus our future – depends on maintaining our integrity. We promote special places – those that add beauty, authenticity and a touch of humanity to our lives. This is a niche, albeit a growing one, so we will spend time pursuing truly special places rather than chasing the mass market.

That said, we do plan to produce more titles as well as to diversify. We are expanding our Go Slow series and have published *Green Europe*, both projects designed to raise the profile of low-impact tourism. Our Fragile Earth imprint is a collection of campaigning books about the environment that will keep you up to date and well-armed for the battle with apathy.

Gwlad beirdd a chantorian
— land of poets and singers.

That is how the Welsh love to think of their Wales, and so do others. If you have ever felt the hairs on your neck rise to the great throated sound of a Welsh male-voice choir, or your heart lift to the lilt of Dylan Thomas's poetry you will understand.

You will know, too, of the ineffable beauty of Wales, a beauty that touches most of the country. From Snowdonia to the Preseli Hills, the beguiling coastal towns to the exquisite Vale of Llangollen and its 15th-century bridge over the Dee, lush green valleys folding one into the other — it is hard to escape the loveliness; the beaches, on the Gower and in Pembrokeshire, are as fine any in the UK.

Yet, I confess, I don't need to dig very deep to find other, less positive, images of Wales: wet sheep gargling on wet hillsides, cold walks in the Brecon Beacons as a parent and cold marches there as a Boy Scout,

the proud tear-filled coal valleys of the south, a 'flat' Welsh response to unnecessary English exuberance.

Then I dig a little deeper and other Welsh images trickle to the surface: porpoises off the Pembrokeshire coast, the puffins on the nearby island of Skomer , the small but big-hearted cathedral of St Davids, the sun above Cadair Idris after a skinny dip in Llyn Cau, descending from the hills to find a wee pub where beer came in jugs from the gnarled hands of a very ancient landlady. There is character a'plenty there.

There is a renewed vigour in Wales today. Is it something to do with having some control over one's own destiny? The Welsh Assembly defies the plodding mediocracy to be found in London, and does its own thing. 'Things' happen now.

Windfarms are erected by communities, and work. Great music is performed in Cardiff, the Welsh National Opera tours and thrives as never before, festivals spring up and blossom, theatres are booming – the Mold Theatre drawing people from all over the North and Midlands. New ideas fall on fertile ground.

My own interests include the environment, and here Wales often leads the way with imaginative policies and rapid execution. The Centre for Alternative Technology is still a pioneer in eco-living and green thinking. Organic farming is encouraged by government, renewable energy schemes are supported, and a clear-sighted view of Wales as responsible for itself is at the heart of it all. Most importantly, perhaps, a powerful sense of community comes with the emphasis on Welsh language teaching. There can be no renewal without community and the Welsh understand this.

Alastair Sawday

Photo: Broniwan, entry 15
Photo right: Penmaenuchaf Hall, entry 49

It's simple. There are no rules, no boxes to tick. We choose places that we like and are fiercely subjective in our choices. We also recognise that one person's idea of special is not necessarily someone else's so there is a huge variety of places, and prices, in the book. Those who are familiar with our Special Places series know that we look for comfort, originality, authenticity, and reject the insincere, the anonymous and the banal. The way guests are treated comes as high on our list as the setting, the architecture, the atmosphere and the food.

Inspections

We visit every place in the guide to get a feel for how both house and owner tick. We don't take a clipboard and we don't have a list of what is acceptable and what is not. Instead, we chat for an hour or so with the owner or manager and look round. It's all very informal, but it gives us an excellent idea of who would enjoy staying there. If the visit happens to be the last of the day, we sometimes stay the night. Once in the book,

properties are re-inspected every few years so that we can keep things fresh and accurate.

Feedback

In between inspections we rely on feedback from our army of readers, as well as from staff members who are encouraged to visit properties across the series. This feedback is invaluable to us and we always follow up on comments.

So do tell us whether your stay has been a joy or not, if the atmosphere was great or stuffy, the owners and staff cheery or bored. The accuracy of the book depends on what you, and our inspectors, tell us. A lot of the new entries in each edition are recommended by our readers, so keep telling us about new places you've discovered too. Please use the forms on our website at www.sawdays.co.uk, or later in this book (page 151).

However, please do not tell us if your starter was cold or the bedside light broken – tell the owner, immediately, and get them to do something about it. Most owners, and staff, are more than happy to correct problems and will bend over backwards to help. Far better than bottling it up and then writing to us a week later!

Subscriptions

Owners pay to appear in our guides. Their fees go towards the high costs of inspecting, of producing an all-colour book and of maintaining our website. We only include places and owners that we find positively special. It is not possible for anyone to buy their way into our guides.

Disclaimer

We make no claims to pure objectivity in choosing these places. They are here simply because we like them. Our opinions and tastes are ours alone and this book is a statement of them; we hope you will share them. We have done our utmost to get our facts right but apologise unreservedly for any mistakes that may have crept in. The latest information we have about each place can be found on our website, www.sawdays.co.uk.

You should know that we don't check such things as fire regulations, swimming pool security or any other laws with which owners of properties receiving paying guests should comply. This is the responsibility of the owners.

Photo right: Peterstone Court, entry 82

Finding the right place for you

Our descriptions are carefully written to help you steer clear of places that will not suit you, but lead you instead to personal paradise. So read between the lines: what we don't say is sometimes as important as what we do.

Wherever you choose to stay, remember that the owners are experts at knowing their patch. They can often recommend secret beaches, excellent restaurants, super walks and gardens to visit — occasionally ones that aren't usually open to the public. Some places may provide maps and a bus timetable; some owners may be happy to pick you up at the end of a long walk. Do ask.

On the B&B pages you will find a huge variety of places, and also owners: some will be hovering with freshly baked cake when you arrive, others may be out shopping for your supper, having left a key under a stone. Mostly these are people's homes; you will encounter family life and its attendant chaos in some, and complete privacy in others, while a fair number of owners will be happy for you to stay all day.

For those who prefer more anonymity, there are many wonderful hotels, some child-friendly, others more suited to those who prefer peace and quiet. A sprinkling of deeply spoiling hotels will keep the fashionistas happy, while there are family-run and comfortingly old-fashioned places for traditionalists. There are also gorgeous self-catering places, some classically contemporary, a few crisply chic, many simple but cosy. Choose from dreamy wilderness boltholes for two, sweet cottages for families, or magnificent houses for larger gatherings.

Maps & directions

Each property is flagged with its entry number on the maps at the front. These maps are the best start to planning your trip, but you'll need a proper road map for real navigation. Most places will send you detailed instructions once you have booked your stay.

Photo : Llys Meddyg, entry 75

Symbols

Below each entry you will see some symbols, which are explained at the very back of the book. They are based on information given to us by owners. However, things do change: bikes may be under repair or WiFi may have been added. Please use the symbols as a guide rather than an absolute statement of fact. Owners occasionally bend their own rules, so it is worth asking if you may take your child or dog, even if the entry doesn't have the symbol.

Children – The 🕴 symbol is given to owners who accept children of any age. It does not mean they will necessarily have cots, highchairs, safety equipment etc, so do check. If an owner welcomes children but only those above a certain age, this is stated at the end of the description. Even these folk may accept your younger child if you are the only guests. Many who say no to children do so not because they don't like them but because they may have a steep stair, an unfenced pond or they find balancing the needs of mixed age groups too challenging.

Pets – The 🐕 symbol is given to places where your pet can sleep in your bedroom but not on the bed. Be realistic about your pet – if it is nervous or excitable or doesn't like the company of other dogs, people, chickens or children, then say so.

Photo left: Penmaenuchaf Hall, entry 49
Photo right: The Grove, entry 66

Rooms

We tell you if bedrooms are doubles, twin/double (ie. with zip and link beds), suite (with a sitting area), family or single. Most owners are flexible and can often juggle beds or bedrooms; talk to them about what you need before you book. Most bedrooms in our B&Bs and hotels have an en suite bath or shower room; we only mention bathroom details when they do not. Please check with owners for bathroom details for self-catering places.

Meals

In B&Bs and hotels a full cooked breakfast is included in the room price, unless we say otherwise.

Obviously if you have chosen to self-cater, you must organise your own. Many of our hotels offer a half-board option, and some of our B&Bs will arrange an evening meal on request.

Bookings and cancellations

Requests for deposits vary; some are non-refundable, and some owners may charge you for the whole of the booked stay in advance.

Some cancellation policies are also more stringent than others. Some will charge you the total cost if you cancel at short notice. If they hold your credit card details they may deduct a cancellation fee from it and not contact you to discuss this. So ask owners to explain their cancellation policy clearly before booking so you understand exactly where you stand; it may well help you avoid a nasty surprise.

Payment

All our owners take cash and UK cheques with a cheque card. Those who also take credit cards have the appropriate symbol.

Photo: Slebach Park, entry 67

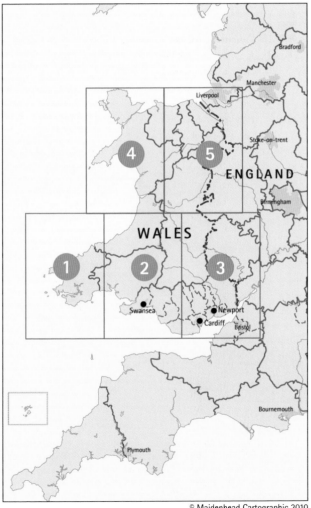

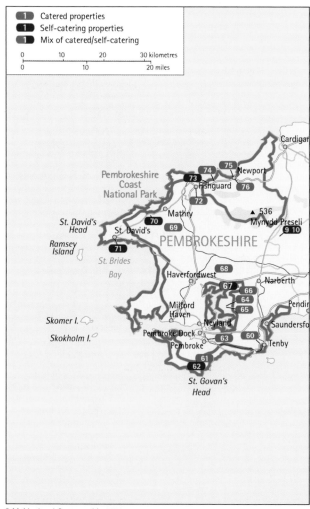

Map 2   19

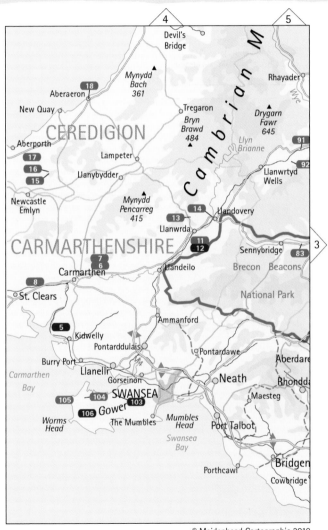

Devil's
Bridge

4   5

Mynydd
Bach
361

Rhayader

Aberaeron   18

New Quay

Tregaron

CEREDIGION

Bryn
Brawd
484

Drygarn
Fawr
645

Aberporth

Lampeter

Llyn
Brianne

91

17
16
15

Llanybydder

Llanwrtyd
Wells

92

Newcastle
Emlyn

Mynydd
Pencarreg
415

14

Llandovery

CARMARTHENSHIRE

13

Llanwrda

11
12

7
6

Llandeilo

Sennybridge

83

Carmarthen

Brecon   Beacons

8

St. Clears

National Park

5

Kidwelly

Ammanford

Burry Port

Pontarddulais

Pontardawe

Llanelli

Carmarthen
Bay

Gorseinon

Neath

Aberdare

Rhondda

105   104

SWANSEA

103

Maesteg

106   Gower

Worms
Head

The Mumbles

Mumbles
Head

Port Talbot

Swansea
Bay

Bridgend

Porthcawl

Cowbridge

Cambrian M

Wye

3

© Maidenhead Cartographic 2010

© Maidenhead Cartographic 2010

Map 4

21

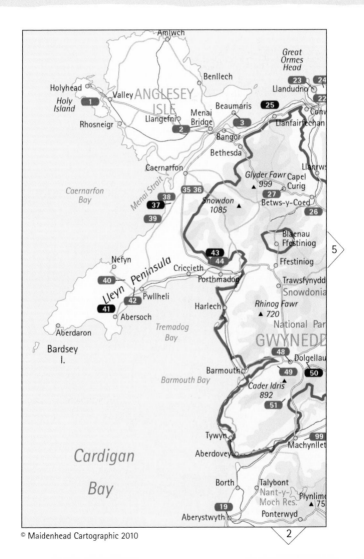

© Maidenhead Cartographic 2010

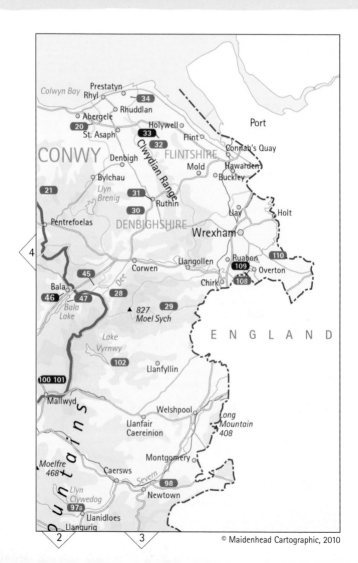

© Maidenhead Cartographic, 2010

Wales

The Seacroft

Big skies, sandy beaches, wheeling gulls, spectacular sunsets – that's what you find at the top of Anglesey. The Seacroft stands just inland, its whitewashed walls sparkling in the sun. It's a very happy place, a pub to some, a restaurant to others. Outside is a decked terrace; inside, New England interiors give an airy seaside feel. Pretty bedrooms are warm and cosy. Two have decked balconies, all come with excellent bathrooms, crisp linen and smart wooden beds. Spin outside to explore and find the wide sands of Trearddur Bay, the coastal path, boats to hire, even a ferry across to Dublin.

Price	£90. Singles from £.75
Rooms	6: 5 doubles, 1 twin.
Meals	Lunch & dinner £5-£30.
Closed	Rarely.
Directions	A55 north onto Anglesey for Holyhead. Exit at junction 2, B4545 into village. Ravenspoint Road signed right after Spar. On right.

Patrick Flynn
Ravenspoint Road, Trearddur Bay LL65 2YU
Tel +44 (0)1407 860348
Web www.theseacroft.com

Neuadd Lwyd

Six sublime acres wrap around you, sheep graze in the fields, views are to a distant Snowdon. This 1871 wisteria-cloaked rectory, has been refurbished in lavish style. The drawing room has deep sofas, polished wood floors, books and a crackling fire; French windows open onto the south-facing terrace. High-ceilinged bedrooms are immaculate and full of beautiful things: cut-glass Venetian mirrors, ornate marble fireplaces, Provençal eiderdowns. Best of all is the cooking. Susannah trained at Ballymaloe so whatever can be is homemade; delicious breads, oatcakes, jams, sorbets, ice creams. Coastal paths will help you atone.

Price	£140–£190. Half-board £97.50–£120 p.p. Singles from £130.
Rooms	4: 3 doubles, 1 twin.
Meals	Dinner, non-residents, £39.50 (not Wednesdays).
Closed	December-January & Sunday-Tuesday throughout year (open bank-holiday Sundays).
Directions	A55 north over Britannia Bridge. 2nd exit for Amlwch, left for Llangefni (B5420). After 2 miles, right for St Gredifael's Church. 1 mile up lane; on right.

Susannah & Peter Woods
Penmynydd, Llanfairpwllgwyngyll LL61 5BX

Tel	+44 (0)1248 715005
Web	www.neuaddlwyd.co.uk

Cleifiog

Liz moved here for the view: you can see why. The creamy Georgian monks' hospice, later an 18th-century customs house, looks across to the whole Snowdon massif – spectacular with the Menai Strait between; the masts of Beaumaris Bay chink in the wind. As well as being a keen gardener, Liz paints and exhibits; her bold, striking pictures are dotted through the house. Big, bright, elegant rooms, are sprinkled with tapestries, antique samplers and fresh flowers. Be charmed by the welcome, the soft linens, the ample breakfasts and the wonderful soft sea air. *Children over three welcome. Minimum stay two nights at weekends.*

Price	£75–£95. Singles £45–£65.
Rooms	3: 2 twins/doubles, 1 suite.
Meals	Pub/restaurant 200 yards.
Closed	Christmas & New Year.
Directions	A55 over Britannia Bridge to Anglesey. A545 to Beaumaris. Past 2 left turns, house is 5th on left facing the sea. Bus stop outside.

Liz Bradley
Townsend, Beaumaris LL58 8BH

Tel +44 (0)1248 811507
Web www.cleifiogbandb.co.uk

Jolyon's Boutique Hotel

Down by the water, the captain's house stands on the oldest residential street in Cardiff Bay. Bang opposite, is the regenerated quayside. At Jolyon's, a boutique hotel run in Mediterranean style, you get spotless, light-flooded (though not huge) bedrooms with creamy walls and colourful fabrics. Find Moroccan lanterns, the odd armoire, Philippe Starck loos in airy bathrooms – in some you can watch TV while you soak in your jacuzzi bath. Drop down to the bar for fresh wood-oven baked pizzas. The feel here is that of a Boston coffee shop, so order an espresso, a local beer or a fancy cocktail, then sink into a leather sofa. *Live music nights and tasting evenings.*

Price	£50–£150.
Rooms	8: 6 doubles, 2 twins.
Meals	Dishes from £2.50. Pizza from £5.50.
Closed	Never.
Directions	M4 junc. 29, then A48(M) for Cardiff. Take exit marked 'Docks and Bay'. Straight ahead, past Millennium Centre & 1st left.

Jolyon Joseph
5 Bute Crescent, Cardiff CF10 5AN
Tel   +44 (0)2920 488775
Web   www.jolyons.co.uk

Gothic Villa

The Bowens have done a great job of restoring this Georgian-style, one-time Customs Office. The result is restfully, stylishly inviting. Tiles, a wood-burning stove, stripped boards, coir matting, and harmonious colours are the backdrop to just-the-right paintings, posters and pottery. Welsh blankets cover the beds, bathrooms are bright and airy. Outside, a pretty garden grows up around a wide, sheltered terrace. Walk the broad, sandy beach at low tide; if you're a railway fan, in the 1840s the line came through and runs between the house and the estuary. The gorgeous gardens of Aberglasney and the Gower's stunning beaches are close.

Price	£650–£1,300 per week. Short breaks £460.
Rooms	Villa for 7: 2 doubles, 1 twin, 1 single.
Meals	Self-catering.
Closed	Never.
Directions	Given on booking.

Entry 5 Map 2

Betsan Bowen
Ferryside SA17 5ST
Tel   +44 (0)1267 267122
Web   www.gothicvilla.co.uk

Plas Alltyferin

Wisteria-wrapped and delightfully creaky in parts, this Georgian family house comes with 270 secluded acres in the handsome Towy Valley, close to the superb gardens of Aberglasney and The National Botanical Gardens. The dining room, where you breakfast, has the original panelling; the bedrooms have an old-fashioned charm. Not the place for you if you like spotlessness and state-of-the-art plumbing, but the views across the ha-ha to the Norman hill fort are timelessly lovely and the welcome is heartfelt. Gerard and Charlotte are the easiest, kindest and dog-friendliest of hosts. *Children over ten welcome.*

Price	£60-£70. Singles £35-£40.
Rooms	2: 1 twin; 1 twin with separate bathroom.
Meals	Pubs/restaurants within 2 miles.
Closed	September & occasionally.
Directions	From Carmarthen A40 east to Pont-ar-gothi. Left before bridge & follow narrow lane for approx. 2 miles keeping to right-hand hedge. House on right, signed. Call for precise details.

Charlotte & Gerard Dent
Pont-ar-gothi, Nantgaredig, Carmarthen SA32 7PF

Tel   +44 (0)1267 290662
Web   www.alltyferin.co.uk

Ty Mawr Country Hotel

Pretty rooms, attractive prices and delicious food make this super country house hard to resist. It's a very peaceful spot. Drive over the hills, drop into the village and wash up at this 16th-century stone house. Outside, a sun-trapping terrace laps against a trim lawn, which drops into a passing river. Inside, stone walls, tiled floors and beamed ceilings give a warm country feel. Excellent bedrooms are all big. You get warm colours, big beds, crisp linen, good bathrooms. Downstairs, the bar doubles as reception, and there's Welsh art on sale. Steve's cooking is the final treat: Cardigan Bay scallops, organic Welsh beef, calvados and cinnamon rice pudding.

Price	£108-£118. Singles from £70. Half-board from £75 p.p.
Rooms	5: 3 doubles, 1 twin/double, 1 twin.
Meals	Dinner £24-£29.
Closed	Rarely.
Directions	M4 west onto A48, then B4310 exit, for National Botanic Gardens, north to Brechfa. In village centre.

Steve Thomas & Annabel Viney
Brechfa SA32 7RA

Tel	+44 (0)1267 202332
Web	www.wales-country-hotel.co.uk

Sarnau Mansion

Listed and Georgian, the house has its own water supply. Play tennis and revel in 16 acres of beautiful grounds complete with pond, walled garden and woodland with nesting red kites. Bedrooms are simply furnished in heritage colours; bathrooms are big. The oak-floored sitting room with chesterfields has French windows onto the garden, the dining room is simpler with separate tables and there's good, fresh home cooking from Cynthia. One mile from the A40, you can hear a slight hum of traffic if the wind is from that direction. You are 15 minutes from the National Botanic Garden of Wales. *Children over five welcome.*

Price	£70–£80. Singles £50.
Rooms	3: 2 doubles, 1 twin.
Meals	Dinner, 3 courses, around £20. BYO. Pub 1 mile.
Closed	Rarely.
Directions	From Carmarthen A40 west for 4 miles. Right for Bancyfelin. After 0.5 miles, right into drive on brow of hill.

Cynthia & David Fernihough
Llysonnen Road, Bancyfelin, Carmarthen SA33 5DZ

Tel +44 (0)1267 211404
Web www.sarnaumansion.co.uk

The Cuckoo House

If the name sounds unique, the place is even more so: the seven-acre estate housed the Protheroe family for centuries. This was the old kitchen, step into an open plan living space clothed in stone, wood and glass. A huge alcove holds a working Victorian range, there's a simple, smart, slate-topped kitchen, a dining table and a staircase leading to basic light-filled bedrooms (and a few squeezed in under the eaves). It's not for the princess and her pea, but most will love the authenticity. Follow the old railway tracks along the river, despite the seclusion you can walk to the pub. Rough, ready, and gloriously eccentric.

Price	£270-£950 per week. Short breaks available.
Rooms	House for 8: 3 doubles, 1 twin.
Meals	Self-catering.
Closed	Never.
Directions	Given on booking.

Jethro Chaplin
Dolwilym, Hebron, Whitland SA34 0YR
Tel   +44 (0)1994 419438
Web   www.selfcateringhouses.com

The Old Bakery

Cocooned in a valley clearing amid giant moss-covered oaks is a relaxed, quirky and wonderful house. Enter a thick-beamed kitchen/diner with flagstones, pipes running along white-plastered walls and the old working bread oven inside an inglenook. Down a few steps is the sitting room: stripy rugs lay about on purple carpet, a sofa and armchairs are there for crashing upon. Two doubles above come without pretension and with colourful throws that will keep your feet toasty. Children will love having their own little sky-lit sleeping space in the loft and you're well-placed for the north and south Pembrokeshire coasts.

Price	£270-£800 per week. Short breaks available.
Rooms	House for 9: 3 doubles, 1 triple.
Meals	Self-catering.
Closed	Never.
Directions	Given on booking.

Jethro Chaplin
Dolwilym, Hebron, Whitland SA34 0YR

Tel	+44 (0)1994 419438
Web	www.selfcateringhouses.com

Entry 10 Map 1

Mandinam

On a heavenly bluff on the edge of the Beacons, beneath wheeling red kites and moody Welsh skies, lies Mandinam, the 'untouched holy place'. Delightful artistic Marcus and Daniella are its guardians, the farm is now mostly conservation land and they look after you as friends. Be charmed by bold rugs on wooden floors, weathered antiques, lofty ceilings, shutters, fires… and scrumptious meals in a red dining room. The serene four-poster room has underfloor heating; the rustic coach house studio is plainer with simple furnishings and shower, a wood-burner and hillside terrace. Watch the sun go down before dinner, revel in the peace. *Minimum stay two nights.*

Price	£70–£80. Singles by arrangement.
Rooms	2: 1 four-poster. Coach house: 1 twin/double.
Meals	Lunch or picnic from £7.50. Dinner with wine, £25. Restaurants & pubs 2 miles.
Closed	Christmas.
Directions	Left at Llangadog village shop; 50 yds, right for Myddfai. Past cemetery, 1st right for Llanddeusant; 1.5 miles, thro' woods on left. Or, by train to Llangadog.

Entry 11 Map 2

Daniella & Marcus Lampard
Llangadog SA19 9LA

Tel	+44 (0)1550 777368
Web	www.mandinam.com

Mandinam: Shepherd's Hut

Four hundred acres of lovingly conserved green, green grass, valley and woodland. Life here is totally detached and a few days on Mandinam farm slows the speed. The Shepherd's Hut – simple, small, warm – plays the part perfectly. Wood coppice fuels the burner, your tiny stove can heat a stew (ask Daniella, she may make you one). The soft bed is on stilts so there's space for your things; there's a sink and a table, too, but eat by the lake if you can. Your outhouse shower is made from reclaimed materials and is solar-powered and wood-heated, and the compost loo feeds the soil so plants flourish. A very sweet retreat.

Price	£70-£80 per night.
Rooms	Cabin for 2 (separate shower & wc).
Meals	Dinner from £20, by arrangement (at farmhouse). Restaurants & pubs 2 miles.
Closed	Christmas.
Directions	Left at Llangadog village shop; 50 yds, right for Myddfai. Past cemetery, 1st right for Llanddeusant; 1.5 miles, thro' woods on left. Or, by train to Llangadog.

Daniella & Marcus Lampard
Llangadog SA19 9LA
Tel   +44 (0)1550 777368
Web   www.mandinam.com

Entry 12 Map 2

Mount Pleasant Farm

Wake up to circling Red Kites with a breathtaking backdrop of the Black Mountain: your bedroom view is one of the best in this book. Sue and Nick are warm and delightful hosts and Sue is a brilliant cook – only the best local lamb and beef will do. The veg is organic and the eggs (deep yellow!) are from up the hill; vegetarians are spoiled too. After dinner there's snooker, a log fire, a cosy sofa; then a seriously comfortable bed in a room with a lovely country-house feel. Aberglasney and the National Botanic Gardens are nearby, coastal walks less than an hour away. *Children over 12 welcome. 1.5 hours from Pembroke Dock.*

Price	£70. Singles £35-£38.
Rooms	3: 1 twin/double; 1 twin/double, 1 single, sharing bath (2nd room let to same party only).
Meals	Dinner, 3 courses with wine £18.50. Packed lunch £7.50.
Closed	Christmas.
Directions	A40 Llandovery-Llandeilo. At Llanwrda, right for Lampeter (A482). Out of village, 1st right after mounted pillar box in lay-by on left. Over bridge & up hill; 1st left. House 1st on right.

Sue, Nick & Alice Thompson
Llanwrda SA19 8AN

Tel +44 (0)1550 777537

The Drovers

The ice-cream pink Georgian townhouse looks good enough to eat – as do the leek and cheese cakes; Jill is a superb cook. A fabulous Welsh hospitality pervades this B&B, along with antiques, gas log fires and peaceful, cosy rooms. Downstairs areas are spacious, with a rambling hotel feel; sunny bedrooms are laced with books and floral wallpapers; bathrooms come in contemporary white and cream, stocked with spoiling towels. Over breakfast (relaxed, delicious, locally sourced) you gaze through deep sash windows onto the town square; order a packed lunch and head for the hills. *Minimum stay two nights at weekends in high season.*

Price	£65-£70. Singles from £45.
Rooms	3: 2 doubles, 1 twin/double.
Meals	Dinner, 3 courses, £20. Packed lunch £5. Inns 50 yds.
Closed	Christmas & New Year.
Directions	In town centre, opposite the fountain.

Jill Blud
9 Market Square, Llandovery SA20 0AB
Tel   +44 (0)1550 721115
Web   www.droversllandovery.co.uk

Broniwan

Carole and Allen have created a model organic farm, and it shows. They are happy, the cows are happy and the kitchen garden is the neatest in Wales. With huge warmth and a tray of Welsh cakes they invite you into their ivy-clad home, cosy and inviting with its warm natural colours and the odd vibrant flourish of local art. Another passion is literature (call to arrange a literary weekend). Tree-creepers, wrens and redstarts nest in the garden, there are views to the Preseli hills, the National Botanic Garden of Wales and Aberglasney are nearby, and the unspoilt coast is a ten-minute drive.

Price	£66–£70. Singles £35.
Rooms	2: 1 double; 1 double with separate bath.
Meals	Dinner £25–£30. BYO. Restaurant 7–8 miles.
Closed	Rarely.
Directions	From Aberaeron, A487 for 6 miles for Brynhoffnant. Left at B4334 to Rhydlewis; left at Post Office & shop, 1st lane on right, then 1st track on right.

Carole & Allen Jacobs
Rhydlewis, Llandysul SA44 5PF

Tel   +44 (0)1239 851261
Web   www.broniwan.com

Rhydlewis House

An 18th-century house in a friendly village with a wealth of nurseries – perfect for gardeners. This ex-drovers' trading post mixes traditional with new: modern furniture by students of John Makepeace, exposed stone walls, rugs on polished wooden floors. The dining room has quarry tiles, an inglenook and Welsh oak cottage-style chairs. A sunny double room with gold curtains overlooks the garden; warm reds, oranges and creams are the colours of the twin. Judith is a terrific cook who uses mostly local produce (Welsh cheeses, an excellent smokery in the village). Single visitors are particularly welcome.

Price	£56-£60. Singles £28-£30.
Rooms	3: 1 double, 1 twin; 1 double with separate bath.
Meals	Dinner £20. BYO. Restaurant 5 miles.
Closed	Christmas.
Directions	North on A487. Right at north side of Sarnau, signed 'Rhydlewis'. T-junc. right to B4334. In Rhydlewis at sharp right bend, left. 40 yards on left.

Judith Russill
Rhydlewis, Llandysul SA44 5PE

Tel	+44 (0)1239 851748
Web	www.rhydlewis-house.co.uk

Ffynnon Fendigaid

Arrive through rolling countryside – birdsong and breeze the only sound; within moments you will be sprawled on a leather sofa admiring modern art and wondering how a little bit of Milan arrived here along with Huw and homemade cake. A place to come and pootle, with no rush; you can stay all day to stroll the fern fringed paths through the acres of wild garden to a lake and a grand bench, or opt for hearty walking. Your bed is big, the colours are soft, the bathrooms are spotless and the food is local – try all the Welsh cheeses. Wide beaches are minutes away, red kites and buzzards soar above you. Pulchritudinous.

Price	From £70. Singles from £40.
Rooms	2 doubles.
Meals	Dinner, 2-3 courses, £15-£18. Packed lunch £6. Pub 1 mile.
Closed	Rarely.
Directions	From A487 Cardigan & Aberystwth coast road, take B4334 at Brynhoffnant towards Rhydlewis. 1 mile to junction where road joins from right & lane to house on left.

Entry 17 Map 2

Huw Davies
Rhydlewis, Llandysul SA44 5SR
Tel   +44 (0)1239 851361
Web   www.ffynnonf.co.uk

Harbourmaster

The harbour at Aberaeron was created in 1807. Shipbuilding flourished and the harbourmaster got his house on the quay with big views over Cardigan Bay. Inside is a winning combination of seductive good looks, informal but attentive service and a menu overflowing with local produce. The airy open-plan dining room/bar has stripped floors and a horseshoe bar, wind up the staircase to super little bedrooms that come with shuttered windows, Frette linen, Welsh wool blankets and quietly funky bathrooms. Borrow a bike and spin off into the hills, coastal paths lead north and south. Sunsets are fabulous. *Minimum stay two nights at weekends.*

Price	£110-£190. Suites £150-£250. Singles £60. Half-board from £80 p.p.
Rooms	13: 11 doubles, 2 singles.
Meals	Lunch from £10.50. Dinner, 3 courses, around £30.
Closed	Christmas Day.
Directions	A487 south from Aberystwyth. In Aberaeron, right for the harbour. Hotel on waterfront.

Glyn & Menna Heulyn
Pen Cei, Aberaeron SA46 0BT
Tel   +44 (0)1545 570755
Web   www.harbour-master.com

Gwesty Cymru Hotel & Restaurant

A seafront gem: a newly refurbished terraced house that overlooks the bay, the pier and Constitution Hill (train up, stroll down). Inside, white walls, Welsh art and Blaenau slate give a fresh contemporary feel. There's a mirrored bar and a cool little restaurant and terrace. Bedrooms are warmly stylish and good value, so splash out on those at the front: leather armchairs face the sea, giving box seats for imperious sunsets, and you get handmade European oak furniture, crisp linen, piles of pillows and silky throws. Bathrooms are magnificent: Italian stone, enormous showers, and double-ended baths: two overlook the bay.

Price	£85–£115. Suite £125. Singles from £65.
Rooms	8: 4 doubles, 3 twins/doubles, 1 single.
Meals	Lunch from £5. Dinner, 3 courses, about £30.
Closed	Rarely.
Directions	On sea front in town close to pier. On-street parking only.

Huw & Beth Roberts
19 Marine Terrace, Aberystwyth SY23 2AZ
Tel   +44 (0)1970 612252
Web   www.gwestycymru.com

The Kinmel Arms

St George is just a handful of cottages – with a sparkling pub-restaurant with rooms. Walk in to a light, open space of cool colours, wood floors and a central bar; then through to a conservatory-style restaurant in cheery yellow, with Tim's pictures on the walls. Food includes Conwy Bay fish, their own lamb, and the bonus of changing guest ales. Behind are four gorgeous suites, each with huge beds and crisp linen, French windows and east facing decking – you breakfast here on goodies from your own fridge. You're a hop from the stunning coast – and Snowdonia – while great walks start from the door. *No children or dogs overnight.*

Price	£115–£175.
Rooms	4 suites.
Meals	Continental breakfast only. Lunch from £6.95. Dinner, 3 courses, about £30.
Closed	Sundays & Mondays.
Directions	A55, junc. 24a from Chester, left up Primrose Hill to village; or junc.24 from Conwy, 1st exit at r'bout onto A547; 1st right towards St George; right onto Primrose Hill.

Tim Watson & Lynn Cunnah-Watson
The Village, St George, Abergele LL22 9BP

Tel	+44 (0)1745 832207
Web	www.thekinmelarms.co.uk

Entry 20 Map 5

The Lion Inn

A simple inn lost in the hills of North Wales – you are more likely to hear birdsong or bleating sheep than a car. In summer, sit at colourful tables on the pavement and watch buzzards circle above, in winter, sip your pint by a fire that burns on both sides in the bar. Downstairs, there are blue carpets and sprigs of hawthorn decorating stone walls. Upstairs, bedrooms are warm and cosy, nicely stylish, super value for money. Breakfasts are big, so burn off the excess on Snowdon or ride your bike through local forests. The mobile reception is useless, the hospitality is magnificent. *Minimum stay two nights at weekends.*

Price	£85. Singles from £53. Family room from £100.
Rooms	5: 2 doubles, 1 twin, 1 single, 1 family room.
Meals	Packed lunches £5. Dinner, 3 courses, about £20.
Closed	Christmas Eve & Christmas Day.
Directions	A55 to Abergele; A544 south to Llansannan; B5384 west to Gwytherin. In village.

Dai Richardson & Rose James
Gwytherin, Abergele LL22 8UU

Tel	+44 (0)1745 860123
Web	www.thelioninn.net

Entry 21 Map 5

The Queen's Head

The old wheelwright's cottage has gone up in the world. It now has low beams, polished tables, walls strewn with old maps and a roaring fire in the bar. The food is home-cooked with a modern twist and generous. The owners have been here for years, nurturing a country local that puts those of Llandudno to shame. Complete the treat by booking a night in the sweet parish storehouse across the road, recently converted into a retreat for two. A gallery bedroom under white-painted eaves, a bathroom lavishly tiled, a small private garden for breakfast – perfect for a romantic break. *The Queen's Head can also be booked for self-catering.*

Price	£100–£150.
Rooms	Cottage for 2.
Meals	Dinner, 3 courses, from £20; Sunday roast £9.25.
Closed	Rarely.
Directions	From A55; A470; right at 3rd r'bout for Penrhyn Bay; 2nd right to Glanwydden after 1.5 miles.

Robert & Sally Cureton
Glanwydden, Llandudno Junction LL31 9JP

Tel   +44 (0)1492 546570
Web   www.queensheadglanwydden.co.uk

Escape Boutique B&B

Llandudno is a holiday town, built by Victorians as a place to take the air. Away from the crowds, Escape stands high on the hill with its carved fireplaces, stained-glass windows and wrought-iron veranda intact. Not that you should expect Victoriana. Interiors have been transformed into a contemporary world of wooden floors, neutral colours, Italian leather and glass chandeliers. Bedrooms — some big, some smaller — come with pillow-top mattresses, goose-down duvets, crisp linen and Farrow & Ball colours. There's an honesty bar and an open fire in the sitting room, while breakfast is a feast. *Minimum stay two nights at weekends.*

Price	£85–£125.
Rooms	9: 8 doubles, 1 twin/double.
Meals	Restaurants & pubs within walking distance.
Closed	Christmas week.
Directions	A55, junc. 19, then A470 for Llandudno. On promenade, head west hugging the coast, then left at Belmont Hotel and house on right.

	Sam Nayar
	48 Church Walks, Llandudno LL30 2HL
Tel	+44 (0)1492 877776
Web	www.escapebandb.co.uk

Lympley Lodge

The solid Victorian exterior belies a surprising interior. Welcoming Patricia, a former restorer, has brought together a gorgeous collection of furniture, while her meticulous paintwork adds light and life to her seaside home. Above is the Little Orme; below, across the main coast road, the sweep of Llandudno Bay. Bedrooms strike the perfect balance between the practical and the exotic; all have crisp linen, rich fabrics, fresh flowers, lovely views. There's an elegant sitting room for guests, a stunning dining room with a Renaissance feel and breakfasts full of local and homemade produce. Wonderful.

Price	£80. Singles £50-£55.
Rooms	3: 2 doubles, 1 twin.
Meals	Restaurants/pubs 5-minute drive.
Closed	Mid-December to end of January.
Directions	From Llandudno Promenade, turn right and follow B5115 (Colwyn Bay) up the hill. Pass right turn for Bryn Y Bia. House entrance (board on side of building) on right.

Patricia Richards
Colwyn Road, Craigside, Llandudno LL30 3AL

Tel   +44 (0)1492 549304
Web   www.lympleylodge.co.uk

Entry 24 Map 4

The Towers

Marvellous to find a house by the beach that sleeps 25! Towers is an ex-harbour master's house, sporting a gothic-style tower with 360 degree views. There are bedrooms galore, from four-posters to bunks, one with a vivid Lady of Shallot mural, another with a Baliese hessian-clad ceiling. The sitting room, overlooking the car park, is turquoise with a domed ceiling painted with stars; and the kitchen, overlooking the garden (with putting green), guards a large range. There's a library, a dining room with a vast table, even a private cinema. In short, a comfortable – and unusual – house suitable for a mix of generations.

Price	£1,643–£3,419 per week.
Rooms	House for 20 (25 with annexe): 2 four-posters, 5 doubles, 2 twins, 1 bunk room for 2, 1 family room, sofabed.
Meals	Self-catering.
Closed	Never.
Directions	Given on booking.

Entry 25 Map 4

Alex Roberts
Llanfairfechon LL33 0DA

Tel   +44 (0)1766 780043

Pengwern Country House

The steeply wooded Conwy valley snakes down to this stone and slate gabled property set back from the road in Snowdonia National Park. Inside has an upbeat traditional feel: a large sitting room with floor-to-ceiling bay windows and pictures by the Betws-y-Coed artists who once lived here. Settle with a book by the wood-burner; Gwawr and Ian know just when to chat and when not. Bedrooms have rough plastered walls, colourful fabrics and super bathrooms, one with a double-ended roll top and views of Lledr Valley. Breakfast on fruits, yogurts, herb rösti, soda bread – gorgeous.
Minimum stay two nights at weekends in summer.

Price	£72–£84. Singles from £62.
Rooms	3: 1 double, 1 four-poster, 1 twin/double.
Meals	Pubs/restaurants within 1.5 miles. Packed lunch £5.50.
Closed	Christmas & New Year.
Directions	From Betws-y-Coed, A5 towards Llangollen for 1 mile. Driveway on left, opp. small stone building.

Gwawr & Ian Mowatt
Allt Dinas, Betws-y-Coed LL24 0HF

Tel	+44 (0)1690 710480
Web	www.snowdoniaaccommodation.co.uk

Entry 26 Map 4

Bryn Tyrch

In the heart of Snowdonia National Park: a no-nonsense mountain retreat for walkers and climbers. Its interior is well-worn, its style laid-back and, best of all, there's a great big blackboard over the fire displaying terrific walkers' food. The goulash is fabulous – served in a mountain of a roll, washed down with a great pint of Orme ale. Picture windows and carefully placed tables in the main bar make the most of the view and there are big brown chesterfields by the fire – arrive early to nab one. Bedrooms are small but beautifully formed: super-comfy beds, big gleaming baths and showers, views worth waking up for.

Price	£40–£110. Singles from £40.
Rooms	12: 10 twins/doubles, 2 bunk rooms.
Meals	Main courses £7.95–£14.95.
Closed	Rarely.
Directions	On A5 near Plas-y-Brenin Mountain Centre, 5 miles west of Betws-y-Coed.

Entry 27 Map 4

Rachel Roberts
Capel Curig, Betws-y-Coed LL24 0EL
Tel   +44 (0)1690 720223
Web   www.bryntyrchinn.co.uk

Tyddyn Llan

A pocket of heaven blissfully lost in imperious country. Everything here is a treat – house, staff, garden and bedrooms. The house stands in three acres with huge views of field and mountain all around. Inside, warm country interiors abound. There's a cavernous sitting room with a roaring fire, eccentric collections of menus and matchboxes in the bar and a wisteria-entwined veranda, where you can eat in good weather. Ambrosial delights await in the candlelit restaurant, so take to the hills and earn your indulgence. Some bedrooms are seriously swanky, but even the simpler rooms elate. Bala, Snowdon and the coast are close.

Price	£110-£200. Suite £260. Half-board from £100 p.p.
Rooms	12: 8 doubles, 3 twins, 1 suite.
Meals	Lunch (Fri & Sat) £21-£28. Dinner £38-£45. Tasting menu £65. Sunday lunch £28.
Closed	Occasionally.
Directions	From A5 west of Corwen, left on B4401 to Llandrillo. Through village, entrance signed right after tight bend.

Bryan & Susan Webb
Llandrillo, Corwen LL21 0ST

Tel	+44 (0)1490 440264
Web	www.tyddynllan.co.uk

The Hand at Llanarmon

Single-track lanes plunge you into the middle of nowhere, lush valleys rise and fall – so pull on your boots. Back at the inn, a coal fire burns in reception, another crackles in the front bar and a wood-burner warms the lofty dining room. Find exposed stone walls, low beamed ceilings, old pine settles and candles on the mantelpiece, a games room, a quiet sitting room for maps and books. Delicious food is popular with locals, stay and you'll get a lovely cooked breakfast. Bedrooms are just as they should be: not too fancy, cosy and warm, with crisp white linen and scrupulously clean. Everyone loves this place.

Price	£85–£120. Singles from £52.50. Half-board from £60 p.p.
Rooms	13: 8 doubles, 4 twins, 1 suite.
Meals	Lunch from £6. Sunday lunch £20. Dinner £12–£20.
Closed	Rarely.
Directions	Leave A5 south of Chirk for B4500. Llanarmon 11 miles on.

Gaynor & Martin De Luchi
Llanarmon Dyffryn Ceiriog, Llangollen LL20 7LD
Tel   +44 (0)1691 600666
Web   www.thehandhotel.co.uk

Entry 29 Map 5

Plas Efenechtyd Cottage

Efenechtyd means 'place of the monks' but there's nothing spartan about Dave and Marilyn's handsome brick farmhouse: breakfasts of local sausages, eggs from their hens, salmon fish cakes with mushrooms and homemade bread, are served at a polished table in the dining room with exotic wall hangings from Vietnam and Laos. Light bedrooms have a clear, uncluttered feel, excellent mattresses and good linen; bathrooms are surprisingly bling and warm as toast with plump towels. Motor or walk to Ruthin with its windy streets and interesting shops, or strike out for Offa's Dyke with a packed lunch; this is stunning countryside.

Price	£60. Singles £40.
Rooms	3: 2 doubles, 1 twin.
Meals	Packed lunch £6. Pub 1.6 miles.
Closed	Rarely.
Directions	From Ruthin follow signs for Bala. Straight over mini roundabout onto B5105. Take first left after 1 mile. Right at T-junction; 50 yds on right.

Dave Jones & Marilyn Jeffery
Efenechtyd, Ruthin LL15 2LP
Tel   +44 (0)1824 704008
Web   www.plas-efenechtyd-cottage.co.uk

Entry 30 Map 5

Manorhaus

Manorhaus is a perfect little townhouse retreat in a sea of lush country. It's Georgian on the outside, groovy within, and doubles as a gallery with contemporary art (all for sale). Downstairs: a white and blue sitting room, a restaurant with wood floors and a small cinema in the Tudor basement. Upstairs: a library for books, maps, CDs, DVDs, and a sauna and steam room to soothe. Bedrooms are funky, some bigger than others, with super bathrooms, oodles of character and big beds with crisp linen and down bedding. Delicious food is fresh and local. Ask about mountain biking, Offa's Dyke is close. *Minimum stay two nights at weekends.*

Price	£95-£125. Suite £150. Half-board £72.50-£95 p.p.
Rooms	8: 7 doubles, 1 suite.
Meals	Dinner, 3 courses, about £29.50.
Closed	Christmas week.
Directions	M56; A55; A494 to Ruthin. Follow signs to town centre, up hill; Well Street on left when entering square.

Christopher Frost & Gavin Harris
10 Well Street, Ruthin LL15 1AH
Tel +44 (0)1824 704830
Web www.manorhaus.com

Plas Penucha

Swing back in time with polished parquet, tidy beams, a huge Elizabethan panelled lounge with books, leather sofas and open fire – a cosy spot for tea in winter. Plas Penucha – 'the big house on the highest point in the parish' – has been in the family for 500 years. Airy, old-fashioned bedrooms have long views across the garden to Offa's Dyke and one has a shower in the corner. The L-shaped dining room has a genuine Arts & Crafts interior; outside, rhododendrons and a rock garden flourish. Beyond is open countryside and St Asaph, with the smallest medieval cathedral in the country.

Price	From £60. Singles from £32.
Rooms	2: 1 double, 1 twin.
Meals	Dinner £18.50. Packed lunch £4.50. Pub 2 miles.
Closed	Rarely.
Directions	From Chester, A55, B5122 left for Caerwys. 1st right into High St. Right at end. 0.75 miles to x-roads & left, then straight for 1 mile. House on left, signed.

Nest Price
Peny Cefn Road, Caerwys, Mold CH7 5BH

Tel	+44 (0)1352 720210
Web	www.plaspenucha.co.uk

Entry 32 Map 5

Gwenoldy

Lambs bleat, swallows swoop – take in the heavenly hill views before stepping through French windows into this converted 18th-century barn. A spotless country kitchen greets you and a living room with oak floors, wood-burning stove and big comfy chairs is perfect after day on Offa's Dyke (less than a mile). Upstairs, the light double room has prettily embroidered white bed linen; beams and primrose walls give the twin a cosy, attic feel. The bathroom is spotless and your pretty, hedged garden, with patio and gas-barbie, has rolling moorland views. Deeply secluded, yet no distance to Snowdonia and magnificent castles.

Price	£330–£500 per week.
Rooms	Cottage for 4: 1 double, 1 twin.
Meals	Self-catering.
Closed	Never.
Directions	Given on booking.

Elizabeth Musgrave
Coed y Mynydd Isaf, Afonwen, Mold CH7 5UU

Tel	+44 (0)1352 720140
Web	www.gwenoldy.com

Golden Grove

Huge, Elizabethan and intriguing – Golden Grove was built by Sir Edward Morgan in 1580. The Queen Anne staircase, oak panelling, faded fabrics and fine family pieces are enhanced by jewel-like colour schemes: rose-pink, indigo, aqua. In summer the magnificent dining room is in use; in the winter the sitting room fire counters the draughts. The two Anns are charming and amusing, dinners are delicious and the family foursome tend the garden – beautiful, productive and well-kept. They also find time for a nuttery and a sheep farm as well as their relaxed B&B. Many return to this exceptional place.

Price	£100. Singles £60.
Rooms	3: 1 double; 1 double, 1 twin, each with separate bath.
Meals	Dinner £28. Pubs within 2 miles.
Closed	November–February.
Directions	Turn off A55 onto A5151 for Prestatyn. At Texaco before Trelawnyd, right. Branch left immed. over 1st x-roads; right at T-junc. Gates 170 yds on left.

**Ann & Mervyn and Ann & Nigel
Steele-Mortimer**
Llanasa, Holywell CH8 9NA

Tel   +44 (0)1745 854452

Entry 34 Map 5

Plas Dinas Country House

This is the family home of Lord Snowdon. It dates to the 1600s and stands in 15 acres with an avenue of oak that sweeps you up to the house. Much of what fills the house belongs to the family: stunning chandeliers, oils by the score, gilt-framed mirrors – an Aladdin's cave of beautiful things. There's a baby grand piano, varnished wood floors, an honesty bar, a fire that roars. Bedrooms are excellent, recently refurbished, the past mixing gracefully with crisp contemporary design. Expect four-posters, cool colours, stylish fabrics. Back downstairs, Andy's cooking hits the spot, perhaps broccoli, port and stilton soup, braised beef with a peppercorn sauce, then Baileys crème brûlée.

Price	£89–£149. Four-posters £129–£199. Singles from £79.
Rooms	10: 4 doubles, 3 twins/doubles, 3 four-posters.
Meals	Dinner, 3 courses, £25–£30.
Closed	22 December–5 January.
Directions	South from Caernarfon on A487. Through Bontnewydd and signed right after half a mile at brow of shallow hill.

Andy & Julian Banner-Price
Bontnewydd, Caernarfon LL54 7YF

Tel	+44 (0)1286 830214
Web	www.plasdinas.co.uk

Entry 35 Map 4

Y Goeden Eirin

A little gem tucked between the sea and the mountains, an education in Welsh culture, and a great place to explore wild Snowdonia, the Llyn pensinsula and the dramatic Eifl mountains. Inside presents a cosy picture: Welsh-language and English books share the shelves, paintings by contemporary Welsh artists enliven the walls, an arty 70s décor mingles with sturdy Welsh oak in the bedrooms – the one in the house the best – and all bathrooms are super. Wonderful food is served alongside the Bechstein in the beamed dining room – the welcoming, thoughtful Eluned and John have created an unusually delightful space.

Price	£80–£100. Singles from £60.
Rooms	3: 2 doubles, 1 twin.
Meals	Dinner, 3 courses, £28. Wine from £14. Packed lunch £12. Pub/restaurant 0.75 miles.
Closed	Christmas to New Year & occasionally.
Directions	From Caernarfon onto Porthmadog & Pwllheli road. A487 thro' Bontnewydd, left at r'bout, signed Dolydd. House 0.5 miles on right, last entrance before garage on left.

Dr John & Mrs Eluned Rowlands
Dolydd, Caernarfon LL54 7EF

Tel	+44 (0)1286 830942
Web	www.ygoedeneirin.co.uk

Entry 36 Map 4

Carmel

Carmel is the second of three cottages facing the bay; cross its little garden and you're on the sand. It's a fabulous site: sunsets are dramatic – watch them from the sitting room's comfortable chairs. You get well-preserved pitch pine floors, a circular Sixties rug, a new-granite fireplace, a desk for budding writers, and good, modern Welsh art on the walls. The terracotta-tiled kitchen has a dining table for four but if you tire of cooking or barbecuing book a delicious dinner at John and Eluned's nearby. Then it's back to Carmel's bedrooms, tiny but snug. Snuggle under the duckdown and let the waves lull you to sleep.

Price	£250-£600 per week.
Rooms	House for 5: 1 double, 1 twin, 1 single.
Meals	Self-catering.
Closed	Rarely.
Directions	Given on booking.

Entry 37 Map 4

John & Mrs Eluned Rowlands
Pontllyfni, Caernarfon LL54 5EG
Tel   +44 (0)1286 830942
Web   www.ygoedeneirin.co.uk

Rhiwafallen Restaurant with Rooms

This intimate restaurant with rooms is one of the best in this far flung, magical landscape. Roll up the drive to old stone walls, ducks on the pond and a pebbled terrace overlooking fields. Inside, cool interiors are warm and restful, but it's the bedrooms that take the biscuit, each one brimming with understated grace. The style is crisply contemporary: Egyptian cotton and down duvets, modern art and flat-screen TVs, fancy bathrooms and fluffy cotton bathrobes. Rob's food is glorious – in summer you eat in a canvas-shaded conservatory with doors onto the terrace. Snowdon is close, as are wild beaches for seaside walks.

Price	£100–£150. Singles from £80.
Rooms	5 doubles.
Meals	Sunday lunch £19.50. Dinner, 3 courses, £35; not Sunday or Monday.
Closed	Rarely.
Directions	South from Caernarfon on A487. Right onto A499 for Llandwrog. Through village and on left after 0.5 miles.

Rob & Kate John
Llandwrog, Caernarfon LL54 5SW

Tel   +44 (0)1286 830172
Web   www.rhiwafallen.co.uk

Y Beuno

This old coaching inn faces the sea with the dramatic Eifl Mountains behind. A long Welsh oak bar sits on slate flags alongside worn polished floorboards, exposed stone and beams, small fires, cosy armchairs. For the adventurous, Purple Moose's Mysterious Myrtle Stout has to be tried, as does Conwy Honey Fayre. The food comes with a Gallic twist courtesy of a Breton chef who does wonders with Caernarfon Bay seafood and lamb from the mountains. Upstairs the treats continue: good-sized bedrooms come with solid wood furniture and sumptuously elegant superior rooms with bathrooms to match: many have views to Anglesey.

Price	£85–£105. Four-posters £135.
Rooms	7: 4 doubles, 2 twins, 1 four-poster.
Meals	Lunch & dinner £5–£30.
Closed	Never.
Directions	In centre of village, set back from A499.

Entry 39 Map 4

Ann Thomas
Clynnog Fawr, Caernarfon LL54 5PB
Tel   +44 (0)1286 660785
Web   www.ybeuno.com

The Old Rectory

In the heart of the Llyn Peninsula, an immaculate Georgian rectory in its own grounds. There are gardens to relax in, a horse in the paddock and wonderful art on the walls – Gabrielle has created delightful interiors. Seagrass floors and toile de Jouy, big mirrors and family antiques, a log fire for cool evenings, a guest drawing room with sofas and books… the mood is one of easy elegance and you can come and go as you please. Gabrielle rides, Roger sails and both are relaxed and charming hosts. The area is stunning, walks start from the door; no wonder guests return. *Pets by arrangement. Minimum stay two nights bank holidays.*

Price	From £90. Singles from £65.
Rooms	3: 2 twins/doubles, 1 double.
Meals	Packed lunch £6.50. Pub/restaurant 2 miles.
Closed	Christmas.
Directions	From Pwllheli, A499 to r'bout. Right onto A497 Nefyn & Boduan road for 3 miles; left opp. church; house set back, on right.

Gabrielle & Roger Pollard
Boduan, Pwllheli LL53 6DT

Tel   +44 (0)1758 721519
Web   www.theoldrectory.net

Entry 40 Map 4

Hen Dy, Nanhoron

People travel miles to see the gardens here, as for Hen Dy, it's the oldest house on the 5,000 acre estate and was the gardener's bothy and laundry, with a bell tower that once announced mealtimes. Now you find a sitting room, large, light and serene, with books, games, soft sofas and SkyTV; in winter, estate logs crackle. The kitchen is made for domestic goddesses, the smart dining room seats eight. Up stairs – or lift – to big restful bedrooms, three of which have garden views. For ball games and barbecues you have your own outside patch – and you are surrounded by the some of most gorgeous countryside in Gwynedd.

Price	£650-£900 per week.
Rooms	House for 7: 1 double, 1 twin/double, 1 twin, 1 single.
Meals	Self-catering.
Closed	Rarely.
Directions	Given on booking.

Bettina Harden
Pwllheli LL53 8DL

Tel   +44 (0)1758 730610
Web   www.nanhoronestate.co.uk

Plas Bodegroes

Close to the end of the world and worth every second it takes to get here. Chris and Gunna are inspirational, their Georgian manor house reached by an avenue of ancient beech trees is a temple of cool elegance, and the food is some of the best in Wales. Not a formal place – come to relax and be yourself. Bedrooms are wonderful, the courtyard rooms especially good, where exposed wooden ceilings give a smart Scandinavian feel. Best of all is the dining room, almost a work of art in itself; cool and crisp with exceptional art on the walls. Don't miss the Lleyn Peninsula: sandy beaches, towering cliffs and country walks.

Price	£110-£175. Singles £50-£99. Half-board from £95 p.p.
Rooms	11: 7 doubles, 2 twins, 1 four-poster, 1 single.
Meals	Sunday lunch £18.50. Dinner £42.50; not Sunday or Monday
Closed	December-February & Sunday & Monday throughout year.
Directions	From Pwllheli, A497 towards Nefyn. House on left after 1 mile, signed.

Chris & Gunna Chown
Efailnewydd, Pwllheli LL53 5TH

Tel   +44 (0)1758 612363
Web   www.bodegroes.co.uk

Entry 42 Map 4

Ynys Pandy

It's beautifully secluded, here in the hills looking into the Snowdonia range. Kind Tomos and Brenda live in one part of the farmhouse, the rest is yours. Cosily furnished, spotlessly clean, you arrive to a warm log burner and fresh scones. In the sitting room are games and books, in the conservatory, comfy chairs and sunshine, in the kitchen, pretty wooden units and crockery – and a scullery with butler's sink and room for wellies. Bathrooms have fluffy towels, bedrooms are colourful with new pine. Children will love the bunks, the grassy garden, climbing frame and swings. Beaches and castles – and Portmerion, are close.

Price	£419-£860 per week. Low season discounts.
Rooms	House for 8: 2 doubles, 1 twin/double, 1 bunk room for 2.
Meals	Self-catering.
Closed	Never.
Directions	Given on booking.

Tomos & Brenda Jenkins
Golan, Garndolbenmaen LL51 9YU

Tel   +44 (0)1766 530256
Web   www.ynyspandy.co.uk

Plas Tan-yr-allt

Who shot Shelley in the drawing room? The poet fled in 1813, the mystery unsolved. The listed house has a colourful history, irresistible to the owners who have just finished a glorious restoration: roll top baths, deep luscious colours, underfloor heating, handsome furniture. *The Daily Telegraph* said Tanny exemplifies "contemporary country-house style"… and there's country-house cooking too. Nick uses local ingredients, and guests eat together at an impressive oak and slate table for dinner – a convivial treat. Wonderful views stretch from the terrace and gardens over the estuary and bay.

Price	£120–£175. Singles £100–£140.
Rooms	6: 3 doubles, 1 twin, 2 four-posters.
Meals	Dinner, 3 courses, £38.50 (Wednesday-Sunday). Pubs/restaurants 10-minute walk.
Closed	4 weeks in January/February.
Directions	Leave Tremadog on A498 for Beddgelert. Signed on left after 0.5 miles. House at top of hill.

Michael Bewick & Nick Golding
Tremadog, Porthmadog LL49 9RG

Tel	+44 (0)1766 514545
Web	www.tanyrallt.co.uk

Dolgadfa

Gasp at the beauty of the road to Dolgadfa, every bend revealing yet another perfect frame of southern Snowdonia – the gentle prelude to the ragged peaks. The youthful Robertsons' slice of this bliss is unexpectedly luxurious. The deep limpid river winds past the listed guest barn where bedrooms – one with stone steps straight onto the riverside garden – are fresh and country-cosy, with gingham curtains and all the trimmings. A bright living room with roaring fire, sofas and Welsh oak floor is yours, and Louise does a fine breakfast. For a couple or a party, a superb place. *Fishing & shooting available.*

Price	£70.
Rooms	3: 1 double, 1 twin; 1 double with separate bath.
Meals	Pub/restaurant in village, 1 mile.
Closed	Christmas.
Directions	B4401; after Llandrillo, 2nd right. Single track road; over bridge; at T-junc. left, on for 1.5 miles; 2nd farmhouse on left. White gate.

Louise Robertson
Llandderfel, Bala LL23 7RE

Tel	+44 (0)7708 249537
Web	www.dolgadfa.co.uk

Abercelyn Country House

The 1729 rectory comes with rhododendron-rich grounds, an immaculate kitchen garden and a mountain stream. In spite of the rugged setting Abercelyn is a genteel retreat. Shutters gleam, logs glow and bedrooms are spacious and light with smart bathrooms and luscious views. You are well looked after: the drawing room overflows with outdoor guides, Ray orchestrates adventure trips to Snowdonia National Park and Lindsay cooks a great breakfast with eggs from their own hens. Bala Lake is a ten-minute stroll – or you can strike off round it for the whole 14 miles – bracing indeed! *Guided walks & canoeing. Self-catering barns available.*

Price	£70–£80. Singles £50.
Rooms	3: 2 doubles, 1 twin/double.
Meals	Pub 10-minute drive. Restaurant 15-min walk; free return taxi service.
Closed	Rarely.
Directions	On A494 Bala-Dolgellau road, 1 mile from centre of Bala, opp. Llanycil Church. Bus service: Wrexham - Bala - Llanycil - Dolgellau - Bamouth.

Ray & Lindsay Hind
Llanycil, Bala LL23 7YF

Tel	+44 (0)1678 521109
Web	www.abercelyn.co.uk

Bryniau Golau

Under clear skies, there are few more soul-lifting views: the long lake and miles of Snowdonia National Park. Each generous room is beautifully furnished – traditional with a contemporary twist, and more glorious views to the garden and lake. Katrina, friendly and adaptable, spoils you with open fires in the sitting room, goose down duvets on the beds, spa baths, underfloor heating and scrumptious breakfasts that set you up for the day. Linger on the lawn, perhaps with a drink as the sun sets, and try your hand at fly fishing or white water rafting. A wonderful place for a house party – and the walking is superb.

Price	£80-£90. Singles £55-£65.
Rooms	3: 2 four-posters, 1 twin/double.
Meals	Supper available. Pubs/restaurants within 2 miles.
Closed	Rarely.
Directions	From Bala B4391; 1 mile, B4403 Llangower. Pass Bala Lake Hotel; look for sign showing left turn; 20 yds after tree, sign on right; left up hill, over cattle grid; 1st on right.

Katrina le Saux
Llangower, Bala LL23 7BT
Tel   +44 (0)1678 521782
Web   www.bryniau-golau.co.uk

Entry 47 Map 5

Ffynnon

An indulging boutique B&B hidden in the backstreets of this old market town. Cycle forested hills, walk white beaches, there are rivers, castles, even Snowdon to climb. If you fail to budge, enjoy the luxury. The exterior may be a tad stern, but inside sparkles: open fires, Farrow & Ball tones, chandeliers and rugs on stripped floors. Breakfast, in the elegant dining room, is communal, there's an honesty bar in the airy sitting room and bedrooms upstairs are magnificent. Expect beautiful beds, high ceilings, elegant fabrics and flat-screen TV/DVDs. Faultless bathrooms are addictive, so expect to go home smelling of roses.

Price	£120–£180. Singles from £80.
Rooms	5: 4 doubles, 1 twin/double.
Meals	Restaurants within walking distance.
Closed	Occasionally.
Directions	Leave A470 for Dolgellau, over bridge, into town. At T-junction, right then 1st left. Straight across Springfield Road & 2nd right into Bryn Teg. Entrance at end of road.

Debra Harris & Steve Holt
Brynffynnon, Dolgellau LL40 1RR

Tel	+44 (0)1341 421774
Web	www.ffynnontownhouse.com

Entry 48 Map 4

Penmaenuchaf Hall

The house has attitude, perched imperiously on the hill, built for a Bolton cotton merchant in 1865. The gardens are amazing — woodlands strewn with daffodils in spring, topiary on the upper lawn, a walled garden of tumbling colour. The smell of woodsmoke greets you at the front door; step inside to find a half-panelled hall with armchairs and a roaring fire, a drawing room with mullioned windows and an elegant upstairs dining room with a terrace for candle-lit summer meals. Bedrooms come in traditional style — one has a balcony and all have good bathrooms. There's excellent fishing, and Snowdon, Bala and Portmeirion are close.

Price	£140–£230. Singles from £95.
Rooms	14: 7 doubles, 5 twins/doubles, 1 four-poster, 1 family room.
Meals	Lunch from £6. Afternoon tea from £6.75. Dinner, 3 courses, £40.
Closed	Rarely.
Directions	From Dolgellau, A493 west for about 1.5 miles. Entrance on left.

Entry 49 Map 4

Mark Watson & Lorraine Fielding
Penmaenpool, Dolgellau LL40 1YB
Tel   +44 (0)1341 422129
Web   www.penhall.co.uk

The Barn, Braich-y-Ceunant

The Barn is heaven for walkers, couples (perhaps with a baby) or anyone in love with lazy, fireside evenings. Modest, simple, genuinely cosy, it's all you need after the long Torrent Walk that passes the owner's house next door. Downstairs, Douglas Fir and time-worn larch beams mix with white-painted stone walls. French windows lead onto a tiny walled patio with unbroken views across the valley, and a wood-burning stove flings warmth across the living room and well-equipped kitchenette. Climb a steep spiral staircase to the open, galleried bedroom – a lofty, airy space with a valley view and simple shower room. Perfect.

Price	£295 per week. Short breaks £195.
Rooms	Barn for 2: 1 double.
Meals	Self-catering.
Closed	Rarely.
Directions	Given on booking.

Chris & Diz West
Brithdir, Dolgellau LL40 2RG
Tel   +44 (0)1341 423345

The Old Rectory on the lake

The drive to get here is fantastic and the approach truly beautiful – The Old Rectory waits for you on the other side of the lake. The owners are full of enthusiasm for their fabulous B&B and spoil guests rotten – comfy beds with smooth Egyptian cotton sheets, binoculars for bird spotting and luxurious baths. Fabulous photos of mountains and lake decorate the dining room, there are views from every window to the luminous lake, and you can climb Cadair Idris from the front door. Return, weak-limbed, to a delicious, home-cooked meal and a bit of cosseting... maybe a wallow in the hot tub under the stars. *Minimum stay two nights at weekends.*

Price	£90. Singles £60.
Rooms	3 doubles.
Meals	Dinner £25. Pub 4 miles.
Closed	Rarely.
Directions	A470 from Dolgellau. A487 from Cross Foxes Inn, then B4405 (signposted Tywyn). Follow along lakeside; right at head of lake and cont. 0.25 miles. House illuminated by blue lights at night.

Entry 51 Map 4

	Ricky Francis
	Talyllyn LL36 9AJ
Tel	+44 (0)1654 782225
Web	www.rectoryonthelake.co.uk

The Gatehouse

How often does one get the chance to stay in a Grade II*-listed gatehouse built by Sir Bogo de Knovil, hunting buddy of Edward I? A steep spiral stone stair leads to a lofty, galleried living space with a wood-burner, fresh modern kitchen, sparkling white wetroom and bedroom on a mezzanine… then spirals to a dressing room above, and then up again to the roof of the tower. From here views stretch to the Wye Valley, the Severn, and, right below, the Tudor manor house, and walled, lawned garden that is yours to share. There's a pub in the village and, at Whitebrook, the Michelin-starred Crown. A perfect romantic bolthole.

Price	£265 per week. Short breaks £180.
Rooms	Gatehouse for 2: 1 double.
Meals	Self-catering.
Closed	Rarely.
Directions	Given on booking.

Juliet Grayson & William Ayot
Moynes Court, Mathern, Chepstow NP16 6HZ

Tel   +44 (0)1291 638806
Web   www.welshgatehouse.com

Entry 52 Map 3

The Nurtons

Following the glorious Wye valley to Adrian and Elsa's history-rich home. The facade is Victorian, the interior rambling and intriguing. This is an old house practising eco-friendly techniques; your hosts are professional ecologists. At the back are two basic B&B suites, with private sitting areas inside and out; a double room is in the main part of the house. Bed linen is air dried, toiletries are mostly Ecover. The price reflects the simplicity, the plantsman's garden reflects a passion for all things organic and you breakfast well – not on bacon and eggs, but fresh fruits, homebaked bread, muesli, honey from their bees.

Price	From £65. Singles from £35.
Rooms	3: 1 double, 1 double & sitting room & child bed, 1 twin & sitting room & sofabed.
Meals	Evening platter £30 (for 2) with glass of wine. Packed lunch £5. Pub 0.75 miles.
Closed	Rarely.
Directions	A466 just north of Tintern village. Drive to house is opposite Old Station Tintern.

Adrian & Elsa Wood
Tintern NP16 7NX

Tel	+44 (0)1291 689253
Web	www.thenurtons.co.uk

Entry 53 Map 3

The White Hart Village Inn

They say T S Eliot visited in 1935; this is his "white hart over the white well" in *Usk*. It is now a food-centred Inn, handsomely revamped. The bar is traditional with exposed stonework and black-painted beams, cushioned settles and a huge 16th-century fireplace. You eat local and seasonal food in one of two rooms: one is traditional, one is contemporary. Up a private stair are two cosy bedrooms with nice firm mattresses on attractively dressed pine beds. There's a mini-kitchen for a continental breakfast that is brought up to you: croissants, cheeses, fresh fruit. So linger or leave early, take a local walk, return for Sunday lunch.

Price	£80.
Rooms	2: 1 double, 1 single.
Meals	Dinner, 3 courses, from £18. Sunday lunch £13.95–£15.95..
Closed	Rarely.
Directions	M4 junc. 25 onto B4596 (Caerleon Rd); through Caerleon village centre on High St, over r'bout onto Usk Rd. On to Llangybi.

David Pell
Llangybi, Usk NP15 1NP

Tel	+44 (0)1633 450258
Web	www.whitehartvillageinn.com

Entry 54 Map 3

Allt-y-bela

A beautiful and ancient house, built between 1420 and 1599, kicking off an early Renaissance architectural buzz and now perfectly restored for the 21st century. It is reached down a narrow lane in its own private and secluded valley. Here is made-to-measure pampering among soaring beams and period furniture. A log-warmed dining room for private meals delivered by two clever chefs, and a big farmhouse kitchen if you want to be more involved. Bedrooms soothe with limewashed walls, fabulous beds, no TV, stunning art, and proper bathrooms. A wonderful retreat that you won't forget.

Price	£125.
Rooms	2 doubles.
Meals	Farmhouse supper £30. Any other meals by arrangement. Pubs/restaurants 3 miles.
Closed	Rarely.
Directions	A449 towards Usk, then B4235 to Chepstow. After 200 yds, unsigned right turn. Follow for 0.5 miles; left into 'No Through Road', follow for 0.5 miles.

William Collinson & Arne Maynard
Llangwm Ucha, Usk NP15 1EZ

Tel	+44(0)7892 403 103
Web	www.alltybela.co.uk

The Beaufort Arms

There's no missing the gracious old coaching inn on Raglan's High Street, with its south-facing terrace at the front. Inside are leather and wicker-arm chairs, open fires, slate floors, cosy corners and a brilliant buzz. Choose from boarded menus in the big bar or pick the brasserie for something fancier. To drink: local ales, Belgian beers, New World wines, French coffee. Bedrooms in the house are inviting and stylish, most have country and church views, all come with white linen, down duvets and pretty throws. (Stable rooms are simpler, smaller and less expensive.) The medieval castle is close, as are the Brecon Beacons.

Price	£60-£105.
Rooms	15 + 1: 8 doubles, 5 twins, 2 singles. Apartment for 2.
Meals	Dinner, 3 courses, from £19.50. Sunday lunch.
Closed	Christmas Day & Boxing Day eve.
Directions	At junction of A40/A449 between Monmouth & Abergavenny. 0.25 miles into village, opp. church.

Eliot & Jana Lewis
High Street, Raglan, Usk NP15 2DY

Tel +44 (0)1291 690412
Web www.beaufortraglan.co.uk

Entry 56 Map 3

The Crown at Whitebrook

An unbeatable combination of attentive service, sublime food and impeccable style make this a real find for those seeking affordable luxury. The Crown is a small restaurant with rooms in a tiny village wrapped up in the Wye Valley. Walks start from the front door, climb the ridge for imperious views or head south to Tintern Abbey. Bedrooms are a treat, seriously comfortable, with crisp linen, pretty colours, decanters of sherry and fluffy white robes – splash out on bigger ones if you can. As for the food, it's Michelin-starred and utterly delicious. Whatever can be is homemade and flavour floods from every bite. Superb.

Price	£115-£140. Singles from £80. Half-board (Monday-Thursday only) from £87.50 p.p.
Rooms	8: 6 doubles, 2 twins/doubles.
Meals	Lunch from £25. Dinner 3 courses, £45. Tasting menus £55-£70. Not Sunday evening.
Closed	Two weeks over Christmas.
Directions	M4 junc. 24, A449/A40 north to Monmouth, then B4293 south. Up hill. After 2.7 miles left for Whitebook. On right after two miles.

David Hennigan
Whitebrook, Monmouth NP25 4TX

Tel	+44 (0)1600 860254
Web	www.crownatwhitebrook.co.uk

The Bell at Skenfrith

A sublime spot by an ancient stone bridge, the inn dates to the 17th century, but its interiors ooze chic. In the locals' bar you find slate floors, open fires, plump-cushioned armchairs. In summer, doors fly open and life decants onto the terrace at the back; priceless views of wood and hill are uninterrupted. Stripped boards in the restaurant give an airy feel, so stop for delicious food served by young, attentive staff. Bedrooms above are dressed in fine fabrics, uncluttered and elegant, brimming with light. Circular walks start from the front door and sweep you into blissful hills. *Minimum stay two nights at weekends.*

Price	£110-£170. Four-posters £195-£220. Singles from £75 (Sunday-Thursday).
Rooms	11: 6 doubles, 2 twins, 3 four-posters.
Meals	Bar lunch from £14. Sunday lunch, 3 courses, £23. Dinner, à la carte, about £30.
Closed	Last week in Jan & first week in Feb.
Directions	From Monmouth, B4233 to Rockfield; B4347 for 5 miles; right on B4521, Skenfrith 1 mile.

William & Janet Hutchings
Skenfrith, Abergavenny NP7 8UH

Tel   +44 (0)1600 750235
Web   www.skenfrith.co.uk

Entry 58 Map 3

Penpergwm Lodge

On the edge of the Brecon Beacons, a large and lovely Edwardian house. Breakfast round the mahogany table, relax by the fire in the sitting room with books to read and piano to play. The Boyles have been here for years and pour much of their energy into three beautiful acres of parterre and potager, orchard and flowers. Bedrooms are gloriously traditional – ancestral portraits, embroidered bed covers, big windows, good chintz – with garden views; bathrooms are a skip across the landing. A pool and tennis for the sporty, two summer houses for the dreamy, a good pub you can walk to. Splendid, old-fashioned B&B.

Price	£70-£75. Singles £40.
Rooms	2 twins, each with separate bath.
Meals	Pub within walking distance.
Closed	Rarely.
Directions	A40 to Abergavenny; at big r'bout on SE edge of town, B4598 to Usk for 2.5 miles. Left at King of Prussia pub, up small lane; house 200 yds on left.

Entry 59 Map 3

Tel
Web

Catriona Boyle
Abergavenny NP7 9AS
+44 (0)1873 840208
www.penplants.com

Penally Abbey

A fabulous position for this 1790 house up on the hill with huge views of Carmarthen Bay to the front; sink into a chesterfield in front of the fire and gaze out to sea. Sprawling lawns are yours to roam and the coastal path passes through. Return to grand four-posters and wild flock wallpaper in the main house; a simpler cottage feel in the coach house; warm contemporary luxury in St Deiniol's Lodge. Steve's gentle, unflappable manner is infectious and hugely relaxing, Elleen cooks in the French style, much of it picked up in the kitchen of a château many years ago; try Tenby sea bass. *Minimum stay two nights at weekends.*

Price	£150–£245. Half-board from £105 p.p.
	Singles from £138.
Rooms	17: Main house: 6 doubles, 1 twin all en suite;
	1 double with separate bath. Coach house:
	4 doubles. Lodge: 5 twins/doubles.
Meals	Lunch by arrangement. Dinner, 3 courses, £36.
Closed	Never.
Directions	From Tenby, A4139 for Pembroke. Right into Penally,
	1.5 miles. Signed at green. Train station 5 mins walk.

	Steve & Elleen Warren
	Penally, Tenby SA70 7PY
Tel	+44 (0)1834 843033
Web	www.penally-abbey.com

Stackpole Inn

In the lovely Stackpole National Park, a jolly, thriving, dining pub with enthusiastic owners and a chef with great local food connections: try Welsh blue cheese pots with crusty bread and local pork in an apple and cider cream sauce. Whiskies, wines and ales are good, too. Rustic rooms come with a mix of exposed beams and stonework, carpets and slate floors, all warmed with wood-burners. Bedrooms are in a separate building and all are light and airy with a contemporary feel; family rooms are good value. Walk the coastal path, climb, fish or surf; each room has a locker for outdoor equipment and there's a cycle rack.

Price	£80-£90. Singles from £55.
Rooms	4: 2 twins/doubles, 2 family rooms.
Meals	Lunch from £5. Dinner, 3 courses, £20-£25 (not Sun eves October-March).
Closed	Rarely.
Directions	B4319 south of Pembroke for 3 miles, then left for Stackpole. Through Stackpole Cheriton, up hill, right at T-junction. On right.

Gary & Becky Evans
Stackpole, Pembroke SA71 5DF

Tel	+44 (0)1646 672324
Web	www.stackpoleinn.co.uk

The Schoolroom Cottage

Steps from the famous Lily Ponds is an irresistible bolthole for two – or three: bring your dog or your child. The cottage is attached to the handsome rectory, all contemporary and charming: a fat sofa, easy chair, books, a cosy wood-burner and a pretty pine table. Dreamy colours remind you that the sea is close, eggs from the family's hens nestle in a basket on the kitchen's beautiful sycamore worktops. Your bedroom has a fabulous big bed and next door is a stylish bathroom. Chase the sun or the shade in your patch of garden; and, just beyond: a jolly pub, a café for teas and a 20 minute walk to a very fine sand beach.

Price	£330-£490 per week.
Rooms	Cottage for 2 (4 with extra bed).
Meals	Self-catering.
Closed	Rarely.
Directions	Given on booking.

Melanie Boissevain
Bosherton, Pembroke SA71 5DN
Tel   +44 (0)1646 661787
Web   www.schoolroomcottage.co.uk

Entry 62 Map 1

Penfro

This is fun – idiosyncratic and a tad theatrical, rather than conventional and uniformly stylish. The Lappins' home is a tall, impressive Grade II*-listed Georgian affair, formerly a ballet school. Judith's taste – she's also a WW1 expert – is eclectic verging on the wacky and she minds that guests are comfortable and well-fed. You eat communally, and very well, at the big scrubbed table in the flagged, Aga-fired kitchen at garden level… the garden's big and beautiful so enjoy its conversational terrace and hammocks. And discuss which of the three very characterful bedrooms will suit you best, plumbing and all!

Price	£65-£90. Singles from £45.
Rooms	3: 1 double;
	1 double, 1 twin both with separate bathroom.
Meals	Packed lunch from £8. Pub 250 yds.
Closed	Rarely.
Directions	A4075 Pembroke; 2 miles to mini r'bout. Straight ahead, down hill, bear right. Right lane past castle; T-junc. bear right. Road widens by Chapel Pembroke Antique Centre. House on right.

Entry 63 Map 1

Judith Lappin
111 Main Street, Pembroke SA71 4DB

Tel	+44 (0)1646 682753
Web	www.penfro.co.uk

Knowles Farm

The Cleddau estuary winds its way around this 1,000-acre organic farm – its lush grasses feed the cows that produce milk for the renowned Rachel's yoghurt. Your hosts love the area, are passionate about its conservation and let you come and go as you please; picnic in the garden, wander through bluebell woods, discover a pond – dogs love it too! Gini rustles up scrumptious, candlelit dinners; food is fully organic or very local (five miles!). You have your own entrance to bedrooms which are old-fashioned but well-maintained, with comfy beds, fresh flowers and glorious views. Traditional, real-farmhouse B&B.

Price	From £65.
Rooms	3: 2 doubles; 1 twin with separate bath.
Meals	Supper from £12. Dinner, 4 courses, £22. Packed lunch £6. Pub 1.5 miles, restaurant 3 miles.
Closed	Rarely.
Directions	A4075 to Cresselly; turn right. Follow signs for Lawrenny to first x-roads; straight over; next x-roads right; 100 yds on left.

Virginia Lort Phillips
Lawrenny SA68 0PX

Tel +44 (0)1834 891221
Web www.lawrenny.org.uk

Entry 64 Map 1

Furzehill Farm

Val and Paul's recently built farmhouse is a friendly and characterful place for families and walkers. The Aga-driven kitchen is the hub and Paul will do you a grand breakfast, and something tasty and local for supper too. There are hunting prints, a modern leather sofa and a brick-surround open fire in the sitting room, and cosy carpeted bedrooms upstairs — one with a shower, two sharing a jazzy jacuzzi. Eco credentials include ground-sourced heating and the young garden promises an above-ground pool. This is a deeply rural spot with a good pub to walk to and the birds of the lovely Cleddau Estuary to admire.

Price	£60–£90. Singles from £30.
Rooms	3: 1 family for 4 or 5; 1 double, 1 room with bunk beds, sharing separate bath.
Meals	Dinner, 3 courses, £18. Supper from £12. Packed lunch £5. Pub/restaurant 3 miles.
Closed	Christmas Day.
Directions	A40 to Canaston Bridge; A4075 for Pembroke. Right at Crosshands; after sharp bend, left for C. Quay; left again at T-junc. for C. Quay; 2nd on left.

Entry 65 Map 1

	E V Rees Martletwy, Narberth SA67 8AN
Tel	+44 (0)1834 891480
Web	www.furzehillfarm.com

The Grove

This handsome Georgian house is lost in Pembrokeshire's hills. Big views shoot off towards the Preselis, wooded hills curl around you, a carpet of bluebells bursts out in Spring. Neil and Zoe have refurbished in great style and their fine Arts & Crafts home mixes old and new to intoxicating effect. You get an explosion of wood in the entrance hall, a roaring fire in the bar and a panelled restaurant for modern country cooking. Bedrooms are split between the main house and converted outbuildings. All are divine, with cool wallpaper, painted armoires, crisp white linen and super-comfy mattresses. Bathrooms are equally spoiling. The coastal path waits for blistering walks.

Price	£140–£210. Suites £220–£260. Singles from £130.
Rooms	12: 8 doubles, 1 twin/double, 3 suites.
Meals	Lunch from £10. Dinner, 3 courses, £25–£35.
Closed	Never.
Directions	M4, then A48 & A40 west towards Haverfordwest. At A470 roundabout, take 1st exit to Narberth. Follow road past Herons Brook. On right, signed.

Neil Kedward & Zoe Agar
Molleston, Narberth SA67 8BX

Tel   +44 (0)1834 860915
Web   www.thegrove-narberth.co.uk

Slebech Park

An imperious position on the Daucleddau Estuary, part of an estate that dates to 1760. You may think you've washed up at the main house, but incredibly, this crenellated building served as the mill and stables. It stands 30 paces from the water with views of river, wood and sky. Each apartment comes with a super kitchen, but there's a rather good restaurant too. Apartments are sublime: grand yet contemporary, 21st-century country-house chic. You get vast sofas, window seats, beautiful colours and fabrics, huge beds, fancy bathrooms. Elsewhere, breathtaking gardens, the ruins of a 12th-century church and a courtyard where you can eat in summer. A perfect place.

Price	£120-£185. Suites £210-£285.
Rooms	7 apartments: 1 for 2, 5 for 4, 1 for 8. Cottage for 4.
Meals	Light lunches from £8.50. Dinner, 3 courses, £20-£30.
Closed	Never.
Directions	M4, then A48 & A40 west. Through Slebech (5 miles east of Haverfordwest) and 1st left. Lodge on left after a mile.

   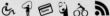

Geoffrey & Georgina Phillips
Slebech, Haverfordwest SA62 4AX

Tel	+44 (0)1437 752000
Web	www.slebech.co.uk

Entry 67 Map 1

Boulston Manor

A lush descent through ancient woodland, with tantalising glimpses of open water, takes you to the ivy-clad 1790s house and a great place to stay. A country-house drawing room with veranda and Cleddau views is yours to use; soft sofas, horsey pictures, fresh flowers and a grand piano set the tone. Perfectly refurbished bedrooms and bathrooms are roomy and glamorous: yards of thick fabrics, dazzling white linen, stone fireplaces, marble tiling, and, in one, a jacuzzi with the grandest parkland views. Generous Jules and Rod are lively and fun, you will eat good, local food and there's miles of walking in the National Park.

Price	£60–£100.
Rooms	3 doubles.
Meals	Supper £15. Dinner from £25.
Closed	Never.
Directions	From Salutation Square (County Hotel) Haverfordwest, take Uzmaston Road past Popes Garage. Through Uzmaston, past Goodwood (signed Boulston). Continue for 1.5 miles and follow Boulston signs.

Roderick Thomas
Haverfordwest SA62 4AQ

Tel	+44 (0)1437 764600
Web	www.boulstonmanor.co.uk

Stone Hall Hotel & Restaurant

A magical 13th-century house lost in sublime country and ten acres of enchanted gardens with lawns, rhododendrons, bluebells, even a handkerchief tree. Heavy beams and stone floors are all original. More recent additions include Nina Campbell wallpaper, pillars, wood carvings and a rather good Venetian Red stone walled bar. Bedrooms are simple, very comfortable, filled with pretty things – perhaps a mirrored armoire, a padded headboard or floral fabrics – and pay no heed to prevailing fashions. Roast away in front of a roaring fire, Martine serves delicious French food. The coast is on your doorstep, fabulous walking abounds.

Price	£105. Singles £75.
Rooms	4: 3 doubles, 1 twin.
Meals	Dinner, 3 courses, £30–£35 (not Sunday or Monday).
Closed	Occasionally.
Directions	A40 north from Haverfordwest. Left for Welsh Hook after Wolf's Castle. Keep left, under railway, over river, past church. Left up hill, signed.

Martine Watson
Wolfscastle, Haverfordwest SA62 5NS

| Tel | +44 (0)1348 840212 |
| Web | www.stonehall-mansion.co.uk |

The Long Barn Cottages

Come for stunning views of the sea and perfect peace. Here are beautifully renovated farm buildings – the Carthouse for six and three cottages in the clematis-strewn barn. Interiors are open-plan and attractive with whitewashed walls, Persian rugs, antique furniture and traditional fabrics. French windows open onto private little gardens, and a big communal one beyond. Older children will delight in stargazing through the velux windows in the Hayloft's bedroom, reached via sturdy ships' ladder. Outside, coastal footpaths radiate and rabbits, badgers and birdlife abound. Gorgeous and secluded.

Price	£300–£760 per week.
Rooms	Piggery for 3: 1 double, 1 single.
	Hayloft/Housemartins for 4: 1 double, 1 twin in each.
	Carthouse for 6: 1 double, 1 twin, bunk room for 2.
Meals	Self-catering.
Closed	February.
Directions	Given on booking.

Helen Zeitlin
Rhoslanogfach, Mathry, Haverfordwest

Tel	+44 (0)1348 837100
Web	www.rhoslanogfach.co.uk

Bwthyn Lil

In the bustling, miniature city of St David's is a stone-built holiday cottage, the oldest of a cluster of three. From its upper floor you can spy the famous cathedral and gaze across open country to the sea. Enter through a royal blue door to find a simple living room enclosed by bumpy, white-washed stone walls and low beamed ceilings — neat and cosy with bright sofas and colourful rugs on a polished wood floor. Eat in the kitchen/diner, at a wooden table in a snug alcove. Upstairs, bedrooms share the same calm cottage style with white linen and pine. It's ten minutes to the coastal path and stunning Whitesand Bay.

Price	£330–£745 per week. Winter short breaks available.
Rooms	Cottage for 3: 1 double, 1 single.
Meals	Self-catering.
Closed	Never.
Directions	Given on booking.

Hamish Elvidge
8 Goat Street, St David's SA62 6RF
Tel +44 (0)1252 842706
Web www.tygwilymholidaycottages.co.uk

Pentower

Curl up with a cat and watch the ferries – or sometimes a porpoise – coasting to Ireland; French windows open onto the terrace and a glorious vista. Mary and Tony are welcoming; they've done an excellent restoration on the turreted 1898 house, keeping its quarry tiled floors, decorative fireplaces and impressive staircase. Spotless bedrooms are light and airy, with large showers; the Tower Room has the views. There's a tiled dining/sitting room for full English (or Welsh) breakfasts – also with views, a 'temple' in the garden for summer, Fishguard is a short stroll, and the stunning coastal path is nearby.

Price	£70–£75. Singles £45.
Rooms	3: 2 doubles, 1 twin.
Meals	Packed lunch £5. Pubs/restaurants 500 yds.
Closed	Occasionally.
Directions	A40 to Fishguard town; at r'bout, 2nd exit onto Main Street. Before sharp left bend, right fork onto Tower Hill; 200 yds on, through house gates.

Tony Jacobs & Mary Geraldine Casey
Tower Hill, Fishguard SA65 9LA

Tel   +44 (0)1348 874462
Web   www.pentower.co.uk

Entry 72 Map 1

33 & 35 Quay Street

These stone built fisherman's cottages have sat on the quayside gazing south across the harbour for 300 years. Boats bob, rigging chinks and the water laps at the sea wall. Step through a front door onto cool terracotta tiles. Living spaces have wood-burners, a wall of books and comfy sofas; dining areas have big convivial tables, and the kitchens are modern and well-fitted. After washing away the last stubborn grain of sand, flop out in fresh bright bedrooms – some overlook the harbour, the gentle susurration of the sea drifting in through open windows. Coastal walks and beaches are close, shops are a stroll away. Lovely.

Price	£315-£680 per week.
	Low season short breaks available.
Rooms	No. 33 for 5: 1 double, 1 twin, 1 single.
	No. 35 for 6: 2 doubles, 1 twin.
Meals	Self-catering.
Closed	Never.
Directions	Given on booking.

Nicholas Yorke
Fishguard SA65 9NB

Tel +44 (0)1239 891180
Web www.quaystreetcottages.com

Entry 73 Map 1

Merton Hall

In front of this intriguing triple-peaked Victorian house lies manicured parkland; behind, a wild, wonderful hill offering stunning sea views. Nigel and Rowena are busy refurbishing Dinas's 'Ty Hen' (Old House), which was pieced together over centuries. Family heirlooms (with matching anecdotes) and naval prints and paintings give the sitting room a certain charm; the dining area's bay windows overlook distant gorse-covered hills. On sunny mornings, join the birds for breakfast in a pretty wisteria-strewn courtyard. You can walk to Aberbach cove, explore the Preseli hills, return to comfortable beds and capable, caring hosts.

Price	£70–£90. Singles £45–£55.
Rooms	2: 1 double, 1 twin.
Meals	Packed lunch for walkers £5. Pub 0.75 miles; restaurants 3.5 miles.
Closed	Christmas, New Year & occasionally.
Directions	From Fishguard, A487 towards Cardigan. After 3 miles enter Dinas Cross. Turn left down track just after 30 limit sign. House is on left after 50 yds.

Rowena Corlett
Dinas Cross, Newport SA42 0XN
Tel +44 (0)1348 811223
Web www.mertonhall.co.uk

Entry 74 Map 1

Llys Meddyg

This quirky restaurant with rooms has a bit of everything: rooms that pack a designer punch, super food in a sparkling restaurant, a cellar bar for drinks before dinner, a fabulous garden with a mountain-fed stream. Inside, Victorian interiors have a warm contemporary finish. Excellent bedrooms are split between the main house (high ceilings) and the news behind (quieter), and come with Farrow & Ball colours, good art, oak beds with crisp linen, fancy bathrooms with fluffy robes. In summer tuck into steak and chips the garden bistro. Don't miss the coastal path for its windswept cliffs, sandy beaches and secluded coves.

Price	£100–£150. Singles from £85.
Rooms	8: 4 doubles, 4 twins/doubles.
Meals	Lunch from £7 (June to mid-Sept). Dinner, 3 courses, about £35; not Sunday/Monday in winter.
Closed	Never.
Directions	East from Fishguard on A487. On left in Newport towards eastern edge of town.

Louise & Edward Sykes
East Street, Newport SA42 0SY

Tel   +44 (0)1239 820008
Web   www.llysmeddyg.com

Cnapan Restaurant & Hotel

Cnapan is a way of life – a family affair with two generations at work in harmony; locals pop in and guests chat in the bar before dinner. It's warm and cosy, charmingly home-spun – whitewashed walls and old pine settles in the dining room; comfy sofas and a wood-burner in the sitting room. There are maps for walkers, bird books, flower books, the daily papers. Spill into the garden in summer for pre-dinner drinks then slip back in for Judith's delicious food. Comfy bedrooms, warmly simple, are super value for money. You're in the Pembrokeshire National Park; beaches and cliff-tops beckon. *Minimum stay two nights at weekends.*

Price	£88. Singles from £54.
Rooms	5: 1 double, 3 twins, 1 family room. Extra bath available.
Meals	Dinner £23–£28. Not Tuesday evenings (Easter to October).
Closed	Christmas, January & February.
Directions	From Cardigan, A487 to Newport. 1st pink house on right.

Eluned Lloyd & Michael & Judith Cooper
East Street, Newport SA42 0SY

Tel   +44 (0)1239 820575
Web   www.cnapan.co.uk

Entry 76 Map 1

Llangattock Court

Built in 1690 and mentioned in Pevsner as an 'outstanding example of a country house in this style', this is indeed grand and sits in the middle of the sleepy village, surrounded by a large garden. Both bedrooms are a good size (one has a big French bed and a small shower room) with lovely antiques and a fresh feel; views from one soar across to the Black Mountains. Breakfast in style in the enormous dining room overlooked by framed relatives, stroll through the rose garden, visit a castle or historic house, walk to the local pub for dinner. Morgan is a painter; some of his paintings are on display.

Price	£50–£80. Singles £45.
Rooms	2: 1 double, 1 suite with four-poster and twin.
Meals	Restaurants/pubs within 1 mile.
Closed	Christmas & New Year; 1–2 weeks October.
Directions	From A465 take B4777 into Gilwern, follow signs to Crickhowell. In Legar, left at Vine Tree Inn. Pass Horse Shoe Inn on right; after 60 yds turn right, then right again 50 yds beyond church signed to Dardy. 1st on left.

Polly Llewellyn
Llangattock, Crickhowell NP8 1PH

Tel	+44 (0)1873 810116
Web	www.llangattockcourt.co.uk

The Coach House and Gardener's Cottage, Glangrwyney Court

Two peaceful hideaways tucked into four acres of beautiful gardens; both crisp, sweet and newly converted in creams, yellows and natural toned carpeting throughout. In the Coach House, pretty country-style units, a Rayburn and modern appliances make self-catering a joy, while bedrooms have a feminine French touch. Sink into immaculate sofas with a DVD or book. Flowers, good linen, superb mattresses and en suite bathrooms are a given here, thanks to bubbly Christina, whose attention to detail is remarkable. Play tennis, take a gin and tonic to the gardens, roam the parkland. The Brecon Beacons and Black Mountains are close.

Price	£350–£550 per week.
Rooms	Coach House for 4: 1 double, 1 twin/double.
	Gardener's Cottage for 4: 2 doubles.
Meals	Self-catering.
Closed	Never.
Directions	Given on booking.

Christina Jackson
Crickhowell NP8 1ES

Tel	+44 (0)1873 811288
Web	www.breconbeaconcottages.co.uk

Ty'r Chanter

Warmth, colour, children and activity: this house is fun. Tiggy welcomes you like family; help collect eggs, feed the lambs or the pony, drop your shoes by the fire. The farmhouse and barn are stylishly relaxed; deep sofas, tartan throws, heaps of books, views to the Brecon Beacons and Black Mountains. Bedrooms are soft, simple sanctuaries with Jo Malone bathroom treats. Children's rooms zing with murals; toys, kids' sitting room, sandpit – child heaven. Walk, fish, canoe, book-browse in Hay or stroll the estate. Homemade cakes, whisky to help yourself to: fine hospitality.

Price	£90. Singles £55.
Rooms	4: 1 double; 1 double with separate bath/shower; 2 children's rooms.
Meals	Packed lunch £8. Pub 1 mile.
Closed	Christmas.
Directions	From Crickhowell, A40 towards Brecon. 2 miles left at Gliffaes Hotel sign. 2 miles, past hotel, house is 600 yds on right.

Tiggy Pettifer
Gliffaes, Crickhowell NP8 1RL

Tel	+44 (0)1874 731144
Web	www.tyrchanter.com

Gliffaes Hotel

A matchless country house with huge views, so sit on the stone terrace and drink it all in; there are 33 acres of conservation woodland and compost-fed gardens so nothing to disturb the absolute peace. Afternoon tea is laid out in the panelled sitting room with its family portraits and crackling log fire, fishermen gather in the bar for tall stories then spin through to the restaurant for locally-sourced seasonal food. Smart, traditional bedrooms, some with river views, one with a claw-foot bath, all have thick fabrics, wool-lined curtains and antiques. Come to cast a fly in the rushing Usk. *Minimum stay two nights at weekends.*

Price	£97–£227. Singles from £85. Half-board from £82 p.p.
Rooms	23: 5 doubles, 14 twins/doubles, 4 singles.
Meals	Light lunches from £5. Sunday lunch £18–£24. Dinner, 3 courses, £34.
Closed	January.
Directions	From Crickhowell, A40 west for 2.5 miles. Entrance on left, signed. Hotel 1 mile up winding hill.

James & Susie Suter
Gliffaes Road, Crickhowell NP8 1RH

Tel	+44 (0)1874 730371
Web	www.gliffaeshotel.com

Entry 80 Map 3

The Old Store House

Unbend here with agreeable books, chattering birds, and twinkling Peter, who asks only that you feel at home. Downstairs are a range-warmed kitchen, a sunny conservatory overlooking garden, ducks and canal, and a charmingly ramshackle sitting room with a wood-burner, sofas and a piano – no babbling TV. Bedrooms are large, light and spotless, with more books, soft goose down, new bathrooms, and armchairs facing views. Breakfast, without haste, on toothsome scrambled eggs, local bacon and sausages, blistering coffee. Bliss – but not for those who prefer the comfort of rules. *Minimum stay two nights at weekends.*

Price	£75. Singles £40.
Rooms	4: 3 doubles, 1 twin.
Meals	Packed lunch £4. Pub/restaurant 0.75 miles.
Closed	Rarely.
Directions	From Brecon, Abergavenny A40. After 1 mile, left for Llanfrynach B4558. Cross narrow stone bridge. House is 1.3 miles on right.

Peter Evans
Llanfrynach LD3 7LJ

Tel   +44 (0)1874 665499
Web   www.theoldstorehouse.co.uk

Peterstone Court

Sheep graze to the front, a swimming pool shimmers by an 11th-century church, a sun-trapping dining terrace overlooks the river Usk. Inside, you'll find a panelled sitting room with an open fire, a spa in the vaulted cellars, a brasserie/bar, a formal restaurant where you eat at weekends. Bedrooms mix country-house style with contemporary colours. Rooms in the old stables reach over two floors and have a smart-rustic feel. Those in the main house have grander dimensions, some with high-ceilings and four-poster beds, others with leather headboards and cavernous sofas; all have fine views. Downstairs, much of the food in the restaurant is reared on the hotel's farm, so dig in.

Price	£110–£220. Singles from £90. Half-board from £85 p.p.	
Rooms	12: 3 doubles, 5 twins/doubles, 2 family rooms, 2 suites.	
Meals	Lunch from £5.50. Dinner, 3 courses, £25–£30.	
Closed	Never.	
Directions	A40 north from Abergavenny for Brecon. On left in village, three miles south of Brecon.	

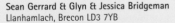

Sean Gerrard & Glyn & Jessica Bridgeman
Llanhamlach, Brecon LD3 7YB

Tel	+44 (0)1874 665387
Web	www.peterstone-court.com

Penpont

A cat idles in the cobbled courtyard. A sheepdog rests with its head on its paws. In your wing you feel private yet part of this great, kindly house. There's a small but comfortable sitting room with an open fire; a big kitchen – candlesticks on a sociably large table, modern units, an old dresser, bold-checked curtains – and the sight and sound of the rushing river. Bedrooms are simple, attractive, with a mix of old furniture, stand-alone basins and plain carpets. This is a cosy and human space, without pretensions, and you feel miles from anywhere. Ask about camping, workshops, conferences, yoga retreats and weddings.

Price	£1,450 per week. Weekend rate £850.
Rooms	Courtyard wing sleeps 15-17 in 6 bedrooms.
Meals	Restaurant 20km.
Closed	Never.
Directions	From Brecon, west on A40 through Llanspyddid. Pass 2nd telephone kiosk on left. Entrance to house on right. Approx. 4.5 miles from Brecon. Sign on right hand side of road.

Entry 83 Map 2

Davina & Gavin Hogg
Brecon LD3 8EU

Tel +44 (0)1874 636202
Web www.penpont.com

The Felin Fach Griffin

It's quirky, homespun, and thrives on a mix of relaxed informality and colourful style; the timber-framed bar has sofas in front of a fire and backgammon waiting to be played. Painted stone walls throughout come in blocks of colour. An open-plan feel sweeps you through to the restaurant; try roasted scallops, Welsh lamb. Bedrooms above are warmly simple and have comfy beds, framed photographs, good books, no TVs (unless you ask). Breakfast is served around one table; make your own toast on the Aga. A road passes outside, quietly at night, lanes lead into the hills, and a small organic kitchen garden provides much for the table.

Price	£105-£150. Singles from £75.
Rooms	7: 2 doubles, 2 twins/doubles, 3 four-posters.
Meals	Lunch £15.90-£18.90. Dinner £21.50-£34.
Closed	24 & 25 December & 4 days in January.
Directions	From Brecon, A470 north to Felin Fach (4.5 miles). On left.

Charles & Edmund Inkin & Julie Bell
Felin Fach, Brecon LD3 0UB

Tel	+44 (0)1874 620111
Web	www.felinfachgriffin.co.uk

Felin Newydd House

A country pad par excellence – on the site of a 17th-century mill, saved from extinction by the owners. Sweeping through the grand hallway, be dazzled by light streaming through the angular cupola. The first to arrive may get the four-poster but each bedroom has its charm – old leather suitcases, polished riding boots – feminine touches in tactile fabrics and glamorous bathrooms. Life revolves around the Aga-toasty kitchen. Supper here – or at a mahogany table in the silk-draped drawing room. Lord and lady it over the 50-acre estate; gorge-walk, fish and canoe. The Brecon Beacons and Black Mountains are close.

Price	£5,750-£8,000 per week. From £1,265 per night.
Rooms	House for 18: 1 four-poster, 4 doubles, 4 twin/doubles.
Meals	Self-catering.
Closed	Rarely.
Directions	Given on booking.

Entry 85 Map 3

	Huw Evans Bevan & Elizabeth Saevareide
	Llandefalle, Brecon LD3 0NE
Tel	+44 (0)1874 754216
Web	www.countrypad.co.uk

The Old Post Office

Unpretentious, simple B&B in the most glorious surroundings. Bedrooms are large, colourful and delightfully quiet; beds are comfortable. Fresh flowers and good books abound, there's a guests' sitting room in which exhausted hikers – and their dogs – can collapse after a recce in the Black Mountains, and it's a two mile walk across fields for all the delights of Hay-on-Wye. Whatever you do, you'll be captivated by the region. Linda serves delicious, cooked vegetarian breakfasts at a long communal table; she and Ed tend to keep to their own part of the house and you come and go as you please.

Price	£70. Singles from £35.
Rooms	3: 1 double, 1 twin/double, 1 double (extra bed).
Meals	Pub 2 miles. Pubs/restaurants in Hay-on-Wye.
Closed	Rarely.
Directions	Hay-on-Wye to Brecon; 0.5 miles, left, signed Llanigon; on for 1 mile, left before school. On right opp. church.

Linda Webb & Ed Moore
Llanigon, Hay-on-Wye HR3 5QA

Tel	+44 (0)1497 820008
Web	www.oldpost-office.co.uk

Entry 86 Map 3

Hideaways in Hay: The Coach House & Stables Cottages

Off a quiet road in Hay, through wooden gates, across a cobbled courtyard with a parterre garden, is a Georgian coach house converted into a lovely hideaway. Plain walls, wooden floors and exposed beams; underfloor heating, a comfy sofa and a wood-burner. The easy living space leads into a kitchen that wants for nothing while downstairs dozes a little bedroom with lacy blinds and wooden shutters front and back, and a bathroom with twin sinks and a sunken bath. Come for the bookshops and literary festival; tick off Offa's Dyke and the mountains. If you have friends, the 12th-century stables next door is an equal treat.

Price	£315–£514 per week. Short breaks available.
Rooms	Coach House for 2 (4 with sofabed): 1 double. Stable Cottage for 2 (4 with sofabed): 1 double.
Meals	Self-catering.
Closed	Rarely.
Directions	Given on booking.

Michael & Séza Eccles
Brook Street, Hay-on-Wye HR3 5BQ
Tel   +44 (0)1497 822827
Web   www.HideawaysInHay.co.uk

Hideaways in Hay: Brookfield House

It's only moments from this bibliophile's 'mecca' to your glorious Jacobean hideaway. The owners sourced everything down to the decorative thunderboxes. There's a handsome lime-plastered dining room and oak steps leading to a kitchen with deep green Victorian shop fittings, marble tops and cut-glass shades: it's pure theatre. En suite bathrooms come with a mosaic tub or surround-sound sauna. The Mistress's bedroom flaunts a curvaceous French wooden bed with lavender-scented sheets; the Master's has a four-poster Indian marriage bed, cast iron bath and walk-in shower. Here is literature, history and finery in equal doses.

Price	£2,000–£3,000 per week.
Rooms	House for 6: 2 doubles, 1 twin.
Meals	Self-catering.
Closed	Rarely.
Directions	Given on booking.

Michael & Séza Eccles
Brook Street, Hay-on-Wye HR3 5BQ
Tel   +44 (0)1497 822827
Web   www.HideawaysInHay.co.uk

Entry 88 Map 3

Hafod Y Garreg

A unique opportunity to stay in the oldest house in Wales – a 1402 cruck-framed hall house, built for Henry IV as a hunting lodge. Annie and John have filled it with a fascinating mix of Venetian mirrors, Indian rugs, pewter plates, gorgeous fabrics and oak furniture. Dine by candlelight – maybe pheasant pie with chilli jam and hazelnut mash: delicious. Bedrooms are stylish and comfortable with Egyptian cotton bed linen. You reach the Grade II*-listed house by a bumpy track across gated fields crowded with chickens, cats, goats, birds… a very special, peaceful and secluded place.

Price	£72. Singles from £68.
Rooms	2 doubles.
Meals	Dinner, 3 courses, £21.50. BYO. Pubs/restaurants 2.5 miles.
Closed	Christmas.
Directions	From Hay-on-Wye, A479 then A470 to B. Wells. Through Llyswen, past forest on left, down hill. Next left for Trericket Mill, then immed. right & up hill. Straight through gate across track to house.

Entry 89 Map 3

Annie & John McKay
Erwood, Builth Wells LD2 3TQ

Tel	+44 (0)1982 560400
Web	www.hafodygarreg.co.uk

Trericket Mill Vegetarian Guesthouse

Part guest house, part bunk house, all very informal – all Grade II*-listed. The dining room has been created amid a jumble of corn-milling machinery: B&B guests, campers and bunkers pile in together to fill hungry bellies with Nicky and Alistair's delicious and plentiful veggie food from a chalkboard menu. Stoves throw out the heat in the flagstoned living rooms with their comfy chairs; the bedrooms are simple pine affairs. Set out to explore from here on foot, horseback, bicycle or canoe; lovers of the outdoors looking for good value and a planet-friendly bias will be in heaven.

Price	£60–£75. Singles £40–£52.50.
Rooms	3: 2 doubles, 1 twin.
Meals	Dinner, 3 courses, £18.50. BYO. Simple supper £8. Pub/restaurant 2 miles.
Closed	Christmas & occasionally in winter.
Directions	12 miles north of Brecon on A470. Mill set slightly back from road, on left, between Llyswen & Erwood. Train to Llandrindod Wells; bus to Brecon every 2 hrs will drop at mill on request.

Alistair & Nicky Legge
Erwood, Builth Wells LD2 3TQ

Tel	+44 (0)1982 560312
Web	www.trericket.co.uk

Rhedyn

Come here if you need to remember how to relax. Such an unassuming little place, but with real character and soul: great comfort too with exposed walls in the bedrooms, funky lighting, pocket sprung mattresses, lovely books to read, and calm colours; bathrooms are modern and delightfully quirky. But the real stars of this show are Muiread and Ciaran: wonderfully warm, enthusiastic and engaging, with a passion for good, local food and a desire for more self-sufficiency – pigs and bees are planned next. This is a totally tranquil place, with agreeable walks through the Irfon valley and bog snorkelling too!

Price	£65. Singles £60.
Rooms	3 doubles.
Meals	Dinner, 3 courses, £25. Packed lunch £7.50. Pub/restaurant 1 mile.
Closed	Rarely.
Directions	From Builth Wells follow A483 towards 'Garth'. Pass Cilmery village, Rhedyn signpost is one mile on right. House is in middle of field.

Muiread & Ciaran O'Connell
Cilmery, Builth Wells LD2 3LH

Tel	+44 (0)1982 551944
Web	www.rhedynguesthouse.co.uk

The Lake Country House & Spa

Deep in the silence of Wales, a country house with a 1920s feel, intent on pampering you rotten: fifty acres of lawns, lake and ancient woodland sweep you clean of city cobwebs, and you come home to afternoon tea in the drawing room, where beautiful rugs warm a brightly polished wooden floor. There are ancient leather-bound fishing logs, grand pianos, grandfather clocks and a snooker table. Dress for a delicious dinner then retire to a smartly traditional or softly contemporary bedroom. Treat yourselves to time in the Spa: the London train takes four hours and stops in the village; resident geese waddle. Marvellous.

Price	£185. Singles from £115-£155. Suites £245-£295. Half-board £105-£150 p.p.
Rooms	30: 6 twins/doubles, 12 suites. Lodge: 12 suites.
Meals	Lunch, 3 courses, £18.50. Dinner, 3 courses, £38.50.
Closed	Rarely.
Directions	From Builth Wells, A483 west for 7 miles to Garth. Signed from village.

Jean-Pierre Mifsud
Llangammarch Wells LD4 4BS

Tel   +44 (0)1591 620202
Web   www.lakecountryhouse.co.uk

The Yat

In a supreme setting of rolling hills studded with sheep is The Yat – a 15th century house where almost everything was reclaimed for restoration; organic wax preserves the floor boards; wool lines the roof. The feel of the house, thanks to charming artist Krystyna, is one of calm, and there are many beautiful things, both modern and antique. Bedrooms are quaint, bathrooms simple. Water is heated by solar thermals, food is almost all organic, breakfasts and suppers scrumptious and local. The garden, formal and wild, tiered and fruit-filled, is a grand place to relax: the only sounds are birdsong and the whispering wind.

Price	£75. Singles from £55.
Rooms	2: 1 double, 1 twin.
Meals	Dinner, 3 courses with wine, £30.
Closed	Rarely.
Directions	Directions from Hundred House village: road to Glascwm, signed at crossroads; at next T-junc., left over humpback bridge; left at next junction; 1st house on right (opp. church).

Krystyna Zaremba
Glascwm, Llandrindod Wells LD1 5SE

Tel +44 (0)1982 570339
Web www.theyat.net

Ffynnonau

Down a mile-long track is a painted wood-clad house, newly landscaped and with sweeping views. Inside are polished floorboards, bold striped furniture, a wood-burner and a cupboard of toys, the feel is fun – thanks to the friendly owners. Explore their farm – 500 acres of it, with ponds for swimming and rabbits, red kites and badgers to spot. The kitchen is a big, well-lit, convivial space, the dining room is gliding distance and the bedrooms, upstairs, are cosy. Two bathrooms have lashings of solar-powered water and Marches views fill every window. Hay is 20 minutes and there are activities galore – including paragliding – on the mountain behind.

Price	£382–£840 per week. Short breaks available.
Rooms	House for 8: 1 double, 2 twins, 1 bunk room for 2.
Meals	Self-catering.
Closed	Never.
Directions	Given on booking.

Natalie Barstow
Hundred House, Llandrindod Wells LD1 5RU

Tel   +44 (0)1982 570736
Web   www.holiday-cottage-mid-wales.co.uk

Entry 94 Map 3

The Swan House

Captivating views of hills, estate and parkland flock to the windows of this immaculate Marches chalet-style bungalow. Shutters give a French twist, a light-hearted hallway greets you with old wooden skis on the wall. Light pours into the sitting room with plenty of snug armchairs, a wood-burner for chilly evenings and a south-facing terrace perfect for deckchair lounging. The kitchen is open-plan and modern, the countryside filters through every pane of the conservatory diner, and bedrooms – in calm blue and green are comfortable and stylish. You get peace, wildlife and the wonderful Offa's Dyke path a footstep away.

Price	£750–£900 per week. Short breaks available.
Rooms	House for 8: 2 doubles, 2 twins.
Meals	Self-catering.
Closed	Never.
Directions	Given on booking.

Penny Morrison
Evenjobb, Powys LD8 2RY

Tel	+44 (0)1547 560460
Web	www.theswanhouse.co.uk

Entry 95 Map 3

The Old Vicarage

Blessed are those who enter… especially devotees of Victoriana. The house, designed by Sir George Gilbert Scott, is a delight. Your host, charming and fun, ushers you in to a rich confection of colours, dark wood and a lifetime's collecting: splendid brass beds, cast-iron radiators, porcelain loos, sumptuous bedspreads and a garden with grotto, waterfall and rill. Dine by candle or gas light (the food is superb), ring the servants' bell for early morning tea. You are on the English side of Offa's Dyke: look north to the heavenly Radnorshire hills, south to all of Herefordshire. *Minimum stay two nights weekends & bank holidays.*

Price	From £98.
Rooms	3: 2 doubles, 1 twin.
Meals	Dinner, 4 courses, £34. Restaurant 10-minute drive.
Closed	Rarely.
Directions	B4355, between Presteigne & Knighton; in village of Norton, immed. north of church.

Paul Gerrard
Norton, Presteigne LD8 2EN

Tel	+44 (0)1544 260038
Web	www.oldvicarage-nortonrads.co.uk

Milebrook House Hotel

An old-school country hotel with three acres of fabulous gardens that run down to the river Teme. Wales is on one bank and England is on the other, so bring your wellies and wade across; the walking is magnificent. Here is a world that's rooted in a delightful past: clocks tick, cats snooze, fires crackle, the odd champagne cork escapes its bondage. Beautiful art hangs on the walls, the sitting room is stuffed with books, and there's food to reckon with in the wonderful dining room. Fish, play croquet, spot kite, deer and kingfishers. Homely bedrooms are more than comfortable, so don't delay. *Minimum stay two nights at weekends.*

Price	£108–£118. Singles from £69. Half-board (min. 2 nights) from £76 p.p.
Rooms	10: 5 doubles, 4 twins, 1 family room.
Meals	Lunch from £9.95. Dinner, 3 courses, £31.95. Not Monday lunchtimes.
Closed	Never.
Directions	From Ludlow, A49 north, then left at Bromfield on A4113 towards Knighton for 10 miles. Hotel on right.

Rodney & Beryl Marsden
Stanage, Knighton LD7 1LT

Tel   +44 (0)1547 528632
Web   www.milebrookhouse.co.uk

The Trewythen Hotel

A small pretty provincial town lost in the mid-Wales hills. The hotel is opposite the town hall, and comes with a little style and lots of comfort. All is spic and span, newly refurbished in neutral colours, with leather sofas and colourful art. Airy bedrooms are very well priced, those at the front on the first floor are huge. All have wooden beds, oatmeal carpets, white walls, good linen, flat-screen TVs and excellent bathrooms (most have showers). Food in the restaurant is simple – pizzas, a good steak, hot apple pie. There's a safe cellar for bikes, fantastic walking, even rally driving – come to try your hand.

Price	£75-£95. Singles from £55.
Rooms	7: 4 doubles, 1 twin, 2 family rooms.
Meals	Lunch from £2.35. Dinner, 3 courses, £17.50. Sunday lunch £14.95.
Closed	Never.
Directions	In centre of town, opposite clock tower.

Huw Griffiths
Great Oak Street, Llanidloes SY18 6BW

Tel	+44 (0)1686 411333
Web	www.trewythen.co.uk

Entry 97a Map 5

The Old Vicarage

Come for vast skies, forested hills and quilted fields that stretch for miles. This Victorian vicarage is a super base: smart, welcoming, full of comforts. You get a log fire in a cosy sitting room, a super-smart dining room with long country views and fancy bedrooms that spoil you all the way. Tim's food is just as good. Local suppliers are noted on menus, but much is grown in the garden, where chickens run free. Resist laziness and take to the hills – the Kerry Ridgeway is on your doorstep as is Powis Castle – for glorious walking, then home and afternoon tea. *Children over 12 welcome.*

Price	£95. Singles £65.
Rooms	3: 1 twin/double, 2 doubles.
Meals	Dinner, 3 courses, £28. Packed lunch available. Pub 4 miles.
Closed	Rarely.
Directions	A483, 3.5 miles from Newtown towards Llandrindod Wells, left on sharp right bend, house first on left.

Tim & Helen Withers
Dolfor, Newtown SY16 4BN

Tel +44 (0)1686 629051
Web www.theoldvicaragedolfor.co.uk

Talbontdrain

Way off the beaten track, remote and wild, sits a white-painted stone farmhouse. The Cambrian mountains stretch to the south, the river Dovey lies in the vale below and kind Hilary knows all the walks and can sort special routes for you. She cooks a hearty breakfast too, or a farmhouse supper, and gives you colourful bedrooms – not swish, but with everything you need. There are photographs of garden plants, a pianola, and furniture in such a mix of styles that it all gives a feeling of great informality. The peace is deep – even the cockerel stays quiet until a respectable time – and walkers will adore it.

Price	£56–£66. Singles £28.
Rooms	4: 1 double, 1 family room for 3; 1 twin/double, 1 single sharing shower.
Meals	Dinner, 2 courses & coffee, £18. Packed lunch £6.
Closed	Christmas & Boxing Day.
Directions	Leaving Machynlleth on A489, 1st right signed Forge. In Forge bear right to Uwchygarreg up 'dead end'. 3 miles, pass phone box on left, up steep hill. House on left at top.

Hilary Matthews
Uwchygarreg, Machynlleth SY20 8RR

Tel   +44 (0)1654 702192
Web www.talbontdrain.co.uk

Entry 99 Map 4

Gesail Farmhouse

Escape to waterfalled valleys – cross a ford and cast civilisation aside. By wild Aran mountains is a much-loved family bolthole. The sitting room is just as it should be – painted stone walls, old beams, a fireplace, blanket-strewn sofas. The dining room snugly seats eight and the kitchen – the old buttery – is a neat space strewn with Welsh slate. Upstairs, bedrooms' floorboards softly creak and slope; while the bathroom, with its painted floorboards and vintage 70s white suite, is quite bohemian. There's no TV, mobiles work at the end of the valley; but, there is a friendly 'spit and sawdust' pub in the village. Super.

Price	£350–£650 per week.
Rooms	House for 6 (8 with extra mattresses): 2 doubles, 2 singles.
Meals	Self-catering.
Closed	Rarely.
Directions	Given on booking.

Mr & Mrs Patrick Minns
Cwm Cywarch, Dinas Mawddwy, Machynlleth SY20

Tel   +44 (0)207 424 0444
Web   www.snowdoniaescapes.co.uk

The Barn, Gesail Farm

Eryri – 'the place of eagles': a fine Welsh name for soaring Snowdonia National Park. From this sheltered hideaway in its south westerly corner, you can stride up mountains or drift along deserted sand dunes. This deeply romantic retreat has it all: stillness and space, fabulous décor and a huge four-poster with a swish bathroom and dressing room. All is open-plan: on whitewashed floorboards in the living space rests a lengthy table alongside a small but perfectly formed kitchen; at the far end, sofas and chairs for lounging – and no TV to distract you from sublime mountain and valley views. A little slice of heaven.

Price	£275-£450 per week.
Rooms	Barn for 2. Extra mattresses and sofabed for up to 6.
Meals	Self-catering.
Closed	Rarely.
Directions	Given on booking.

Mr & Mrs Patrick Minns
Cwm Cywarch, Dinas Mawddwy, Machynlleth SY20 9JG

Tel	+44 (0)207 424 0444
Web	www.snowdoniaescapes.co.uk

Lake Vyrnwy Hotel & Spa

Wedged into the mountains of North Wales, Lake Vyrnwy shimmers under forest and sky. The hotel sits high on the hill with stupendous views stretching five miles north; the sofa in the drawing room must qualify as one of the loveliest places to sit in Wales. Country house bedrooms, most with lake views, are all different: some are snug in the eaves, many have balconies, in one you can soak in a claw-foot bath while gazing down the lake. Elsewhere, a terraced bar, a country pub, a spoiling spa and a super restaurant. Outside, pheasants roam, sheep graze, there's tennis and fishing. *Minimum stay two nights at weekends.*

Price	£120–£210. Singles from £95. Half-board £87.50–£130 p.p.
Rooms	52: 41 twins/doubles, 7 four-posters, 1 suite, 3 singles.
Meals	Lunch from £8.50. Bar meals from £8. Dinner, 5 courses, £39.50.
Closed	Rarely.
Directions	A490 from Welshpool; B4393 to Lake Vyrnwy. Brown signs from A5 at Shrewsbury as well.

The Bisiker Family
Llanwddyn, Oswestry SY10 0LY

Tel   +44 (0)1691 870692
Web   www.lakevyrnwyhotel.co.uk

The Granary

Across the lovely open space of Cefn Bryn ridge, past sheep and wild ponies, is the village of Reynoldston and an old cattle byre with beech floors, oak beams, granite worktops, slate sills – it's won restoration awards. The Granary is airy in summer, cosy in winter (wood-burning stove, chunky shutters). On the ground floor are excellent beds with crisp linen, shower rooms and a vaulted living room/kitchen whose big patio doors open to a terrace with Gower peninsula views; up a spiral stair is a second room with TV and DVD. Friendly owners are next door, you walk to the local pub, and it's a short drive to sandy beaches.

Price	£425-£850 per week.
Rooms	House for 4: 1 double, 1 twin/double.
Meals	Self-catering.
Closed	Never.
Directions	Given on booking.

Paul & Mair Jones
Hayes Farm House, Reynoldston, Swansea SA3 1HN

Tel   +44 (0)1792 391306
Web   www.thegranarygower.co.uk

Entry 103 Map 2

Fairyhill Hotel

Fairyhill is a sublime country house wrapped up in 24 acres of blissful silence. There's a terrace for lunch, a stream-fed lake, an ancient orchard, a walled garden with asparagus beds. Inside is loaded with warmth and colour with an open fire in the bar, a grand piano in the sitting room and super local food in the restaurant; confit of duck and pistachio terrine, local sea bass with scallops and green beans, then apple and tarragon tart with ice cream. Most bedrooms are big and fancy, a couple are small, but sweet. Duck eggs for breakfast, croquet on the lawn and a treatment room for massage. *Minimum stay two nights at weekends.*

Price	£175-£275. Singles from £155. Half-board from £122.50 p.p.
Rooms	8: 3 doubles, 5 twins/doubles.
Meals	Lunch from £9.95. Dinner £35-£45.
Closed	First 3 weeks in January.
Directions	M4 junc. 47, A483 south, then A484 west to Gowerton and B4295 for Llanrhidian. Through Oldwalls, 1 mile up on left.

Andrew Hetherington & Paul Davies
Reynoldston, Swansea SA3 1BS

Tel   +44 (0)1792 390139
Web   www.fairyhill.net

Blas Gwyr

Sleepy Llangennith was once a well-kept secret – now walkers, riders, surfers and beach lovers of all ages flock here. Tucked back from the bustling bay is an extended 1700s cottage with a boutique hotel facelift. All is simple but stylish: bedrooms are modern and matching with tiled floors and contemporary paintings, while bathrooms come with warm floors and fluffy towels. Everything from the bedspread to the breakfast is local: make sure you try the lava bread. After a day at sea fling wet gear in the drying room and linger over a coffee on the front deck, or walk to the pub for a sun-kissed pint. Bliss. *Welsh spoken.*

Price	£100–£110. Singles £85.
Rooms	4: 1 double, 1 double (with sofabed), 1 twin/double, 1 suite for 2-4.
Meals	Packed lunch £5. Dinner £20 (Friday/Saturday, for groups of 6 or more, by arrangement). Pub 150 yds.
Closed	Never.
Directions	In Llangennith, pass pub, at mini r'bout, right, then immed. right.

	Dafydd & Kerry James
	Plenty Farm, Llangennith, Swansea SA3 1HU
Tel	+44 (0)1792 386472
Web	www.blasgwyr.co.uk

Entry 105 Map 2

Oriel Gwyr

A product designer by trade, John has, quite literally, carved out his first house – in the sought-after hamlet of Rhossili. The roof is insulated and grassed over, the odd sun pipe breaks through the turf to funnel light down, and there's an air-source heat pump for the underfloor heating: you'll like the toasty floors. The whole house is muted, immaculate, curvaceous and double glazed. You are three miles from groceries but a local and organic welcome hamper will get you started. A clifftop restaurant is a two-minute stroll and it's a tumble down the path to the sweeping sands of Rhossili beach – one of Wales's finest.

Price	£800–£1,600 per week.
Rooms	House for 8 (3 doubles, 1 twin).
Meals	Restaurant 100 yds.
Closed	Never.
Directions	From Swansea, A4118 to Port Eynon. At Scurlage, right onto B4247 until you reach Rhossili; on right 100m before church.

John Williams
Rhossili SA3 1AU

Tel +44 (0)1792 391425
Web www.orielgwyr.co.uk

Holm House

A glittering hotel by the sea: stylish, intimate and spoiling. Interiors mix Art Deco with contemporary flair. Find half-panelled walls, vintage wallpaper and a mirrored bar/sitting room. Downstairs, doors open onto a balustraded terrace with gardens below and the sea beyond; on a good day you're on the Côte d'Azur. Slip into the airy restaurant for delicious comfort food. Beautiful bedrooms come with Frette linen, super beds, designer fabrics and Italian ceramics in smart bathrooms. There are loungers on a first-floor sun terrace, a spa for treatments and a hydrotherapy pool. Heaven. *Minimum stay two nights at weekends.*

Price	£150-£355. Half-board (obligatory Friday & Saturday) £110-£212.50 p.p.
Rooms	12: 4 suites, 6 doubles, 2 twins.
Meals	Lunch from £14.95. Dinner £23.50-£28.50; weekends, 5 courses, £39.50.
Closed	Never.
Directions	M4 junc. 33, then A4232 south. Follow signs to Penarth town centre (not marina). Along seafront, up hill, 1st right; 4th house on right.

Susan Sessions
Marine Parade, Penarth CF64 3BG

Tel	+44 (0)2920 701572
Web	www.holmhouse.co.uk

The Garden House

Unbelievable that a few years ago this was bare farmland. Simon and Susie have worked magic: Simon building the handsome brick house, his mother transforming the land into a symphony of lawns, boxed hedges, hideaways, a bridged pond with views to the river, sculptures here and there, hordes of hydrangeas, a greenhouse for afternoon tea. One of Simon's passions is art and antiques so inside is equally creative: the smart double room in the main house and separate Orangery suite are bursting with artworks and original pieces. Eat in the wonderfully chaotic family kitchen or walk to the pub, wake to a dawn chorus, revel in the enthusiasm of it all.

Price	£100. Singles £60.
Rooms	2: 1 double with sitting room. Orangerie: 1 double with sitting room.
Meals	Supper £20-£30. Pub/restaurant 0.75 miles.
Closed	Occasionally.
Directions	A483 to Chester, turn on to A539 (Whitchurch). Turn right on A528; right by Cross Foxes pub. Follow Gardens sign. House 0.75 miles on right.

Simon Wingett
Erbistock, Wrexham LL13 0DL

Tel   +44(0)1978 781149
Web   www.simonwingett.com

Wynnstay Hall

At the end of a beech-lined drive is a Grade II-listed Victorian pile in French Renaissance style. Your share has been adventurously revamped into a 21st-century bolthole; the rest is private apartments. A lift takes you to snug attic bedrooms and large sleek mezzanine suites. Downstairs is the Great Hall, oak-panelled with a suit of armour and a vast open-tread staircase. Other sitting areas have huge fireplaces, leather sofas and a bar, a pool table, grand piano and a cinema. Eat range-cooked meals at a long table beneath a glittering chandelier. City escapees will love it – and the Capability Brown landscaped grounds.

Price	£1,500-£3,000 per week.
Rooms	Hall for 18 (20 with sofabed): 7 doubles, 2 twins.
Meals	Self-catering.
Closed	Never.
Directions	Given on booking.

Alex Roberts
Wynnstay Hall Estate, Overton Road,
Ruabon, Wrexham LL14 6LA

Tel   +44 (0)1766 780043

Worthenbury Manor

Homemade bread and Hepplewhite! This is a good, solid house of generous proportions and your hosts live in part of it. Wallow in antique oak four-posters in rose-carpeted chandeliered bedrooms, full of comfort (books, games and flowers adding a cosy touch) and breakfast on fresh fruit (some from the garden) local bacon and sausages. Ian, history buff and former chef, is gentle, thoughtful and looks after you properly; dinner is quite an occasion. The listed house is close to Chester yet in a quiet, birdsung setting; the original building was enlarged in the 1890s in the William and Mary revival style.

Price	£60–£85. Singles £38–£49.
Rooms	2: 1 four-poster; 1 four-poster with separate bath.
Meals	Dinner, 3 courses, £25. Lunch £15.
Closed	December–February.
Directions	Between A525 Whitchurch-Wrexham & A41 Whitchurch-Chester, on B5069 between Bangor-on-Dee (also called Bangor-is-y-coed) and Malpas. Manor on right before bridge.

Elizabeth & Ian Taylor
Worthenbury LL13 0AW

Tel   +44 (0)1948 770342
Web   www.worthenburymanor.co.uk

Ship Inn
Red Wharf Bay
Pentraeth LL75 8RJ

+44 (0)1248 852658
www.shipinnredwharfbay.co.uk

Neil Kenneally

Ship Inn
Red Wharf Bay

The boatmen still walk across from the estuary with their catch. Inside the Ship, fires roar in several fireplaces and bars share nautical bits and bobs. There are pews and benches and bare stone walls, and huge blackboards where the daily specials change almost by the hour. At night, the menu proffers Welsh seafood based on the best the boats have brought in: grilled turbot served with lemon and seasonal vegetables; dressed crab. But the old Ship is so much more – a family-friendly public house where, for 30 years, regulars and visitors have been enjoying great ales and freshly prepared food, from 'brechdanau' – sandwiches – to 'pwdin'. Fine Welsh cheeses, too. These lovely people are as proud of their hospitality as they are of their language – and the vast sea and sand views from the front terraces are inspiring.

Meals	12pm-2.30pm; 6pm-9pm (12pm-9pm Sun). Main courses £7.95-£17.95; bar meals £4.75-£12.95.
Closed	Open all day.
Directions	Off B5025, north of Pentraeth.

One of our favourite Welsh pubs
from our guide *Pubs & Inns of England & Wales*

Y Polyn
Nantgaredig
Carmarthen SA32 7LH
+44 (0)1267 290000
www.ypolynrestaurant.co.uk

Mark & Susan Manson,
Simon & Maryann Wright

Y Polyn
Nantgaredig

The pub sits by a fork in the roads, one leading to Aberglasney, the other to the National Botanic Garden of Wales. This lot know their onions – Susan was head chef at the Worshipful Company of Innholders, Maryann chef-patron at the Four Seasons in Nantgaredig – and have jollied up the interior with bold colours, herringbone matting, local art, fresh flowers and candles. A wicker sofa and armchairs by the fire encourage you to loll, while the restaurant has a happy mix of tables and chairs. The short menu is pleasingly simple: fresh local ingredients well put together. Start with duck and ham hock terrine with piccalilli, move onto crispy roast pork belly with caramelised apples or Welsh lamb hotpot, finish with plum and frangipane tart or rhubarb fool. You are equally welcome to just pop in for a drink.

Meals	12pm-2pm; 7pm-9pm (9.30pm Fri-Sun).
	Main courses £9.50-£15.50 (lunch)' set menus (dinner) £23.50 & £29.50; Sunday lunch £17.50 (2 courses) & £22.50 (3 courses)
Closed	4pm-7pm, Sun eve & Mon all day.
Directions	Off junction of B4300 & B4310 between A48 & A40 east of Carmarthen.

One of our favourite Welsh pubs
from our guide *Pubs & Inns of England & Wales*

The Groes Inn,
Ty'n-y-Groes,
Conwy LL32 8TN

+44 (0)1492 650545
www.groesinn.com

Dawn & Justin Humphreys

The Groes Inn
Conwy

The first licensed house in Wales (1573) is splendidly old-fashioned, with rambling bars, nooks and crannies, and low beams and doorways that demand heads be bowed. Painted stonework is hung with local prints and pictures, there are displays of teacups and Victorian postcards, a red carpet, a polished Welsh dresser, a woodburner to keep things toasty. Our pint of Orme's Best – brewed by Justin's cousin – went down a treat, as did the prime-beef burger in its great toasted bap, with crisp mixed salad and delicious hand-cut chips. In the more elegant restaurant, 32 wines accompany award-winning dishes: baked field mushrooms, Conway crab and Anglesey oysters, sweet Welsh lamb with rich rosemary jus, chocolate-scented pancakes with sumptuous ice cream. For summer: a pretty garden with lovely mountain views. Excellent all round.

Meals	12pm-2.15pm; 6.30pm-9pm; 12pm-9pm Sun. No food Sun eves in winter. Main courses £9.65–£16.85 (bar); £13.25–£24.50 (restaurant); sandwiches (lunch only) from £5.75.
Closed	3pm-6pm. Open all day on Sun in summer.
Directions	A55 to Conwy, then B5106 south for 1.5 miles; hotel on right.

One of our favourite Welsh pubs
from our guide *Pubs & Inns of England & Wales*

The Corn Mill,
Castle Street,
Llangollen LL20 8PN

+44 (0)1978 869555
www.cornmill-llangollen.co.uk

Andrew Barker

The Corn Mill
Llangollen

The 18th century has been left far behind in this renovated corn mill beside the swiftly flowing Dee. Not only is the interior light, airy and well-designed but the busy menu is laced with contemporary ideas. There are also gorgeous views onto the river whether you're quaffing your pint of Phoenix in the fabulous bar, or settling down to eat in one of the upper-floor dining areas. The decked veranda-cum-walkway is stunning, built out over the cascading rapids with a gangway overhanging one end beyond the revolving water wheel. Watch dippers and wagtails as you tuck into smoked haddock and mozzarella rarebit, Welsh pork sausages with spring onion mash, king prawn salad with chilli dressing. The Brunning & Price formula is known for its 'something-for-everyone' appeal, and the setting is supreme.

Meals   12pm-9.30pm (9pm Sun). Main courses £8.95-£16.50.
Closed   Open all day.
Directions Off Castle Street (A539) just south of the river bridge.

One of our favourite Welsh pubs
from our guide *Pubs & Inns of England & Wales*

Plough & Harrow,
Monknash,
Cowbridge CF71 7QQ

+44 (0)1656 890209
www.theploughmonknash.com

Gareth Davies & Alistair Jones

Plough & Harrow
Monknash

Originally part of a monastic grange, and well off the beaten track, today's Plough & Harrow is hugely convivial. Ancient, low white walls lead you to the front door, then you dip into two dim-lit, low-ceilinged, character-oozing rooms, their rustic fireplaces filled with church candles or crackling logs. There are cheerful yellow walls, original floors, church pews, smiling staff and a small bar area with a big array of handpumps – up to 11 ales are served. Traditionalists will be relieved to see gammon and chips on the lunch menu while the more adventurous may plump for summer crab salad, moules marinières and roasted duck breast on potato fritters. A brilliant atmosphere, a great find, the kind of pub you wish was your local – and it is as friendly to single drinkers as it is to groups.

Meals	12pm-2.30pm (12pm-5pm Sat); 6pm-9pm (5pm-8pm Sun).
	Main courses £6.50-£14.95; bar meals £4-£9.50.
Closed	Open all day.
Directions	Village signed off B4265, between St Brides Major & Llantwit Major, 6 miles south west of Cowbridge.

Penhelig Arms,
27-29 Terrace Road,
Aberdyfi LL35 0LT

+44 (0)1654 767215
www.penheligarms.com

Glyn Davies

Penhelig Arms
Aberdyfi

It's small, friendly and rather smart, and the way things are done here is second to none. Village life pours through: old boys drop by for a pint, passing friends stop for a chat, families book in for a birthday lunch. Staff are friendly, and generous prices draw a loyal crowd. Fronting the inn is the tiniest harbour; along the quay come the fishermen, butchers, bakers and smallholders who deliver daily to the kitchen. The food is fabulous and the fish comes straight from the sea. Try hake stew with garlic and chorizo, or fillet steak with peppercorn sauce for carnivores; on sunnier days you can enjoy a refreshing drink and a snack at your chosen spot close to the harbour wall. Local art adorns the walls in the restaurant and a fire burns in the local's bar. Coast and hills beckon – bring the boots.

Meals	12pm-2pm; 7pm-9pm (bar meals from 6pm). Main courses £8.95-£15.95; bar snacks from £4; set dinner £29; Sunday lunch £19.
Closed	3pm-5.30pm (5pm Sat & Sun). Open all day at peak times.
Directions	Through Machynlleth, then A493 to Aberdyfi. Inn on right entering village. Parking opposite.

One of our favourite Welsh pubs
from our guide *Pubs & Inns of England & Wales*

The Hardwick,
Raglan Road, Hardwick,
Abergavenny NP7 9AA

+44 (0)1873 854220
www.thehardwick.co.uk

Stephen Terry

The Hardwick

Hardwick

After working in Marco Pierre White's kitchens, Stephen Terry runs his own show. In the shadows of the Black Mountains, the pub's proximity to The Walnut Tree – which Stephen also owned – has helped put this roadside inn on the gastropub map. The stripped-back-to-basics interior is a modest background for some seriously fine wines and astonishingly good food. While some of the ingredients are imported from Italy, most originate from closer to home – and that includes the Welsh beers on draught. The lengthy menu incorporates Blumenthalian marvels such as thrice-cooked chips, alongside comforting classics (a meltingly rich Longhorn beef pie with oxtail, kidney and ale). Try the set lunch (Tues-Fri), then walk off your indulgence among some of the best landscapes of Wales.

Meals	12pm-3pm; 6.30pm-10pm.
	Main courses £13.25-£23; Sunday lunch £11.50 & £18.50.
Closed	3pm-6pm, Sun eve & Mon all day.
Directions	One mile south-east from Abergavenny via A40 & B4598.
	Call for directions first.

One of our favourite Welsh pubs
from our guide *Pubs & Inns of England & Wales*

The Swan,
Point Road, Little Haven,
Haverfordwest SA62 3UL

+44 (0)1437 781880
www.theswanlittlehaven.co.uk

Paul & Tracey Morris

The Swan
Little Haven

Little Haven is jumbled into the seaward end of a narrow valley with glorious views across St Bride's Bay... trek up the cobbled path to reach the lovely old Swan, whose fabric and fortunes have been restored by Paul Morris. Original features abound in the uncluttered but snug side room and warm blue-painted dining room; imagine bare boards and stone, simple wooden furnishings and glowing stoves for wild winter days. Equally warming is the delicious food: at lunch, homemade soda bread topped with smoked salmon or traditional Welsh cawl with local Caerfai cheese; in the evening, venison with red cabbage and autumn fruits, and bitter chocolate tart. For summer there's a broad wall to lounge on and a tiny terrace, so settle in for the day with a foaming pint of Bass and enjoy the views – they're stupendous.

Meals	12pm-2.00pm; 6pm-9pm.
	Main courses £4.50-£9.90 (lunch), £5.90-£16.90 (dinner).
Closed	Open all day.
Directions	By the quay in the village centre.

One of our favourite Welsh pubs
from our guide *Pubs & Inns of England & Wales*

Nag's Head Inn,
Abercych,
Boncath SA37 0HJ

+44 (0)1239 841200

Sam Jamieson

Nag's Head Inn
Abercych

Behind the vibrant orange exterior is a feast of bare wood and stone. The lighting is soft and warm, there's a rustic chicken-wire sideboard crammed with old beer bottles, a glass cabinet displaying the famous 'rat' of Abercych (a stuffed coypu) and a photo of old Emrys, the treasured regular after whom the home-brewed beer is named. The Nag's Head has a simple, tasteful charm, is full of old tales, curios and quirkery and serves the best kind of hearty pub food, from whitebait and fresh soups to steak and kidney pudding, treacle tart, and delicious Sunday roasts. Come with the family and explore the pushchair-friendly Clynfyw sculpture trail – it starts from here. There's a play area too, in the long, lovely riverside garden. By a bridge on the river bank, at the bottom of a steep hill, the setting alone is worth the trip.

Meals	12pm-2pm; 6pm-9pm.
	Main courses £8-£15.
Closed	3pm-6pm & Mon all day (except bank hols). Open all day Sun.
Directions	Off A4332 between Cenarth & Boncath.

One of our favourite Welsh pubs
from our guide *Pubs & Inns of England & Wales*

The Harp,
Old Radnor,
Presteigne LD8 2RH

+44 (0)1544 350655
www.harpinnradnor.co.uk

Jenny & David Ellison

The Harp
Old Radnor

David and Jenny Ellison bring bags of experience (time spent at Bristol's Hotel du Vin) to this ancient Welsh longhouse tucked up a dead-end lane near the parish church. The wonderful interior is spick-and-span timeless: 14th-century slate flooring in the bar, tongue-and-groove in a tiny room that seats a dozen diners, crannies crammed with memorabilia, an ancient curved settle, an antique reader's chair, two fires and a happy crowd. Enjoy a pint of Shropshire Lass with a Welsh Black rump steak or a tagine of organic lamb with herb couscous, or pan-fried cod with pea and tarragon purée. Or take a ploughman's to a seat under the sycamore and gaze upon the spectacular Radnor Valley for total tranquillity. Life in this tiny village, like its glorious pub, remains delightfully unchanged.

Meals	12pm-2pm (Sat & Sun only); 6.30pm-9pm.
	Main courses £7.95-£15; bar meals £4.25-£6.50.
Closed	Tues-Fri lunch, 3pm-6pm Sat & Sun & Mon all day.
Directions	From Kington A44; after 3 miles left for Old Radnor.

One of our favourite Welsh pubs
from our guide *Pubs & Inns of England & Wales*

Sawday's Travel Club membership opens up hundreds of discounts, treats and other offers in selected B&Bs and hotels in Britain and Ireland, as well as discounts on Sawday's books and other goodies.

Alastair **Sawday's**

re is a little taster of some member offers ailable at participating special places*:

TRAVEL CLUB

- 3 nights for the price of 2
- 25% off room price
- Bottle of champagne on arrival
- Late check-out
- Locally produced chocolates
- Organic Dorset cream tea
- Bottle of wine with dinner
- Trout fishing day on the Tamar
- Cornish pasties and Devonshire chutney on arrival
- Free picnic and maps for walkers

To see membership extras and to register visit:

www.sawdays.co.uk/members

Only £25 per year

*Individual terms and conditions apply
...stair Sawday Publishing accepts no responsibility for any of the Travel Club Offers

Sawday's Gift Cards

Sawday's Gift Cards can be used at a whole array of bed and breakfasts, hotels and pubs with rooms scattered across the British Isles. You may fancy a night in a country house which towers majestically over the River Usk, or perhaps a weekend in a splendid Georgian mansion in the Cotswolds. Stay in a garret above a legendary London coffee house or sample a stunning barn conversion in the depths of Northumberland.

Wherever you choose as a treat for yourself, friends or a loved one we know it will be fun, unusual, maybe even eccentric and definitely life affirming. A perfect present.

They come in four denominations – £25, £50, £75 and £100 and come in attractive packaging, which includes a series of postcards and a printed booklet featuring all the participating places.

You can purchase Gift Cards at: www.sawdays.co.uk/gift-cards/ or you can order them by phone: +44(0)1275 395433.

You can also view the full list of participating places on our website www.sawdays.co.uk and search by this symbol: 🎁

Special places to stay, slow travel and slow food

The Slow Food revolution is upon us and these guides celebrate the Slow philosophy of life with a terrific selection of the places, recipes and people who take their time to enjoy life at its most enriching. In these beautiful books that go beyond the mere 'glossy', you will discover an unusual emphasis on the people who live in Special Slow Places and what they do. You will meet farmers, literary people, wine-makers and craftsmen – all with rich stories to tell. *Go Slow England, Go Slow Italy* and our new title *Go Slow France* celebrate fascinating people, fine architecture, history, landscape and real food.

"*Go Slow England* is a magnificent guidebook" *BBC Good Food Magazine*

RRP £19.99. To order any of these titles at the Readers' Discount price of £13.00 (plus p&tp) call +44(0)1275 395431 and quote 'Reader Discount WAL'.

Have you enjoyed this book? Why not try one of the others in the Special Places series and get 35% discount on the RRP *

British Bed & Breakfast (Ed 14)	RRP £14.99	Offer price £9.75
British Bed & Breakfast for Garden Lovers (Ed 5)	RRP £14.99	Offer price £9.75
British Hotels & Inns (Ed 11)	RRP £14.99	Offer price £9.75
Devon & Cornwall (Ed 1)	RRP £ 9.99	Offer price £6.50
Scotland (Ed 1)	RRP £ 9.99	Offer price £6.50
Pubs & Inns of England & Wales (Ed 6)	RRP £15.99	Offer price £10.40
Ireland (Ed 7)	RRP £12.99	Offer price £8.45
French Bed & Breakfast (Ed 11)	RRP £15.99	Offer price £10.40
French Holiday Homes (Ed 4)	RRP £14.99	Offer price £9.75
French Châteaux & Hotels (Ed 6)	RRP £14.99	Offer price £9.75
French Vineyards (Ed 1)	RRP £19.99	Offer price £13.00
Italy (Ed 5)	RRP £14.99	Offer price £9.75
Spain (Ed 8)	RRP £14.99	Offer price £9.75
Portugal (Ed 4)	RRP £11.99	Offer price £7.80
Morocco (Ed 3)	RRP £ 9.99	Offer price £6.50
India & Sri Lanka (Ed 3)	RRP £11.99	Offer price £7.80
Green Europe (Ed 1)	RRP £11.99	Offer price £7.80
Go Slow England (Ed 1)	RRP £19.99	Offer price £13.00
Go Slow Italy (Ed 1)	RRP £19.99	Offer price £13.00

*postage and packing is added to each order

To order at the Reader's Discount price simply phone
+44 (0)1275 395431 and quote 'Reader Discount WAL'

If you have any comments on entries in this guide, please tell us. If you have a favourite place or a new discovery, please let us know about it. You can return this form to WAL, Sawday's, The Old Farmyard, Yanley Lane, Long Ashton, Bristol BS41 9LR, UK or visit www.sawdays.co.uk.

Existing entry

Property name: ──────────────────────────

Entry number: ────────────── Date of visit: ──────────

New recommendation

Property name: ──────────────────────────

Address: ──────────────────────────

Tel/Email/Website: ──────────────────────────

Your comments

What did you like (or dislike) about this place? Were the people friendly? What was the location like? What sort of food did they serve?

──────────────────────────────────

──────────────────────────────────

──────────────────────────────────

Your details

Name: ──────────────────────────

Address: ──────────────────────────

────────────── Postcode: ──────────

Tel: ────────────── Email: ──────────

Climate Change　Our Warming World　　　£12.99

"Climate Change presents in a clear and unique way the greatest challenge facing humanity. It is illustrated with telling photography and sharply written text. It is both objective and passionate. To read it is to know that urgent action is needed at every level in all societies." *Jonathan Dimbleby*

Climate Change is the greatest challenge facing humaity today. In the coming decade a tipping point may be reached triggering irreversible impacts to our planet. This book is not just for scientists or academics, it is for everyone concerned about the future of the earth .

Also available in the Fragile Earth series:

What About China? Answers to this and other questions about climate change　£6.99
Ban the Plastic Bag A community action plan　£4.99
One Planet Living A guide to enjoying life on our one planet　£4.99
The Little Food Book An explosive account of the food we eat today　£6.99

To order any of the books in the Fragile Earth series call
+44 (0)1275 395431 or visit www.fragile-earth.com

Money Matters
Putting the eco into economics £7.99

This well-timed book will make you look at everything from your bank statements to the coins in your pocket in a whole new way. Author David Boyle sheds new light on our money system and exposes the inequality, greed and instability of the economies that dominate the world's wealth.

Do Humans Dream of Electric Cars
£4.99

This guide provides a no-nonsense approach to sustainable travel and outlines the simple steps needed to achieve a low carbon future. It highlights innovative and imaginative schemes that are already working, such as car clubs and bike sharing.

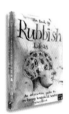

The Book of Rubbish Ideas £6.99

Every householder should have a copy of this guide to reducing household waste and stopping wasteful behaviour. Containing step-by-step projects, the book takes a top-down guided tour through the average family home.

The Big Earth Book
Updated paperback edition £12.99

This book explores environmental, economic and social ideas to save our planet. It helps us understand what is happening to the planet today, exposes the actions of corporations and the lack of action of governments, weighs up new technologies, and champions innovative and viable solutions.

Alastair
Sawday's
British self-catering

A whole week self-catering in Britain with your friends or family is precious, and you dare not get it wrong. To whom do you turn for advice and who on earth do you trust when the web is awash with advice from strangers? We launched Special Escapes to satisfy an obvious need for impartial and trustworthy help – and that is what it provides. The criteria for inclusion are the same as for our books: we have to like the place and the owners. It has, quite simply, to be 'special'. The site, our first online-only publication, is featured on www.thegoodwebguide.com and is growing fast.

Cosy cottages • Manor houses

Tipis • Hilltop bothies

City apartments and more

www.special-escapes.co.uk

1 Conwy   **2** B&B

3 Escape Boutique B&B

4 Llandudno is a holiday town, built by Victorians as a place to take the air. Away from the crowds, Escape stands high on the hill with its carved fireplaces, stained-glass windows and wrought-iron veranda intact. Not that you should expect Victoriana. Interiors have been transformed into a contemporary world of wooden floors, neutral colours, Italian leather and glass chandeliers. Bedrooms – some big, some smaller – come with pillow-top mattresses, goose-down duvets, crisp linen and Farrow & Ball colours. There's an honesty bar and an open fire in the sitting room, while breakfast is a feast. *Minimum stay two nights at weekends.*

Price	£85–£125.	**5**
Rooms	9: 8 doubles, 1 twin/double.	**6**
Meals	Restaurants & pubs within walking distance.	**7**
Closed	Christmas week.	**8**
Directions	A55, junc. 19, then A470 for Llandudno. On promenade, head west hugging the coast, then left at Belmont Hotel and house on right.	**9**

10

Sam Nayar
48 Church Walks, Llandudno LL30 2HL

11 Entry 23 Map 4

Tel   +44 (0)1492 877776
Web   www.escapebandb.co.uk